The Ministry of Teaching

by David and Roberta Plake

GOSPEL PUBLISHING HOUSE
SPRINGFIELD, MISSOURI

02-0567

THE MINISTRY OF TEACHING

This is a Workers Training Division textbook. Credit for its study will be issued under Classification 4, Sunday School Department, Assemblies of God.

Library of Congress Catalog Card Number 82-81509
International Standard Book Number 0-88243-567-1
Printed in the United States of America

Foreword

The awesome responsibility for the propagation of the Christian faith has been committed to the church of Jesus Christ. With this responsibility the Lord has given gifts to His church for the equipping of the saints and the edification of His church. One of the gifts given to the body of Christ is teachers. As we read the Scriptures, we can see that men and women of God were gifted in explaining and teaching the Christian faith.

The strength in many denominations lies in their Sunday school and Christian education departments. The Assemblies of God has benefited from a strong Sunday school emphasis. We have seen the necessity of teaching our children, youth, and adults the principles and practices of our Christian faith.

David and Roberta Plake have compiled and authored a sound, practical, and easy-to-understand book on the subject of teaching and teachers. They have included helpful information that will aid the teacher and anyone else involved in Christian education and the mechanics of teaching. However, this book does not just dwell on the mechanics of teaching, but emphasizes the importance of teaching as a result of a living and loving relationship with Jesus Christ. One can sense the burden of this book as stress is made upon every Sunday school worker having a deep commitment not just to Christian truth, but to the living Saviour! A teacher filled with God's Spirit can have a tremendous impact on his students.

This book should be read by every Sunday school teacher and worker, and anyone who wants to be a better disciple of our Lord. I encourage every pastor to make this book part of his library, and involve his church in the teaching of this workers training course.

RICHARD W. DORTCH
DISTRICT SUPERINTENDENT
ILLINOIS DISTRICT COUNCIL
OF THE ASSEMBLIES OF GOD

Contents

Contents

1

The Ministry of Teaching in the Church

> To this end was I born, and for this cause came I into the world, that I should bear witness unto the truth (John 18:37).

The Great Commission was given to every disciple of Jesus Christ (Matthew 28:19,20). However, unto some is given a special calling, a special gift, of teaching. "When he ascended up on high, he . . . gave gifts unto men. . . . And he gave some, apostles; and some, prophets; and some, evangelists; and some, pastors and teachers" (Ephesians 4:8,11).

The Call

How awesome and marvelous is the call of God! What matchless grace that allows us to become a part of His immutable plan and purpose! God says: "My purpose will stand, and I will do all that I please. . . . I summon . . . from a far-off land, a man to fulfill my purpose. What I have said, that will I bring about; what I have planned, that will I do" (Isaiah 46:10,11, NIV). St. Augustine said: "Without God we cannot. Without us, God will not."

Throughout the Word of God there is record of men and women who have been called and gifted of God for a specific task—David, Jeremiah, Paul, etc. Not only has God chosen men and women of old, but He also continues to look for those who will be used of Him. "Ye have not chosen me, but I have chosen you, and ordained you, that ye should go and bring forth fruit, and that your fruit should remain" (John 15:16).

The Gift

Not only have we been called of God, but also by grace we have been especially gifted of God for our ministries to the body of Jesus Christ. Notice that in Ephesians 4:11 the word "some" does not precede the office of "teacher" as it does the other offices. D. V. Hurst points out that "the original Greek indicates clearly, the ministries of pastor and teacher are combined in one office—pastor-teacher."[1]

Judson Cornwall says:

> It must be pointed out that the last two on the list are combined: "pastors and teachers," since all pastors are required to be "apt to teach" (2 Timothy 2:24). In checking through twenty different translations of the New Testament, I found that all of them combined the final two positions.[2]

Roy B. Zuck observes that teaching is "closely associated with preaching (Acts 5:42; 1 Timothy 2:7; 2 Timothy 1:11), and is closely linked with the gift of pastoring. . . . This implies that one cannot be a true pastor without also being a teacher. . . . The pastor-teacher compares to the 'teaching priest' of the Old Testament (2 Chronicles 15:3)."[3]

Many associate the gift of pastoring with preaching and exhortation, while they associate the gift of teaching with explaining. The gift of pastor-teacher actually encompasses both. Teaching explains, while preaching announces the message and asks for repentance and dedication. However, both effective preaching and teaching contain elements of explanation, announcement, and exhortation.

The effective pastor of a church is deeply involved with the people of his congregation; he feels with them and empathizes with their problems. So it is with the Sunday school teacher and his class of students.

The fact that the gift of pastor-teacher is closely entwined does not say that the *position* of ministry (service) is the same. No Sunday school class teacher should consider himself to be *the* pastor or *the* shepherd of a little flock. God has given both gifts and positions of ministry (see Romans 13:1,2; Hebrews 13:7,17; 1 Peter 5:5).

Is it a natural or a spiritual gift?

> Like other spiritual gifts, it is a supernatural ability. . . . A Christian teacher with the gift of teaching does not necessarily know more about the Word of God than others, but that gift does enable him to impart more effectively that which he does know.[4]

What is the difference between an ability learned in the world before salvation, and that same ability used in the body of Christ after salvation? The difference lies in the results. Natural abilities in the world reap material results, whereas supernatural abilities reap spiritual results. "For he that soweth to his flesh shall of the flesh reap corruption; but he that soweth to the Spirit shall of the Spirit reap life everlasting" (Galatians 6:8).

Certainly there are instances of gifts being given supernaturally to those who have never shown natural abilities in those areas; however, in most cases God enhances natural gifts and channels those abilities into spiritual spheres of ministry.

Aholiab had a natural ability to be an engraver, a skillful craftsman, and an embroiderer (Exodus 38:23). But God put within him and others "wisdom and understanding to know how to work all manner of work for the service of the sanctuary" (Exodus 36:1). God spoke to Moses, saying: "Thou shalt speak unto all that are wise-*hearted*, whom I have filled with the *spirit* of wisdom, that they may make Aaron's garments" (Exodus 28:3). Notice that the wisdom had gone beyond the head into the heart and the spirit for this service unto the Lord.

Before Paul's conversion he had been trained in the schools of his day. God took those natural abilities, quickened them with His spirit, and used him mightily.[5]

The Gift of Teaching in the Church

Teaching is God's established means of proclaiming His

laws and His love. Moses told the people, "These are all the laws that the Lord your God commanded me to teach you" (see Deuteronomy 6:1). After Israel's exile, a whole system of schools, or synagogues, was established. In Jesus' day, the rabbi, or teacher, was held in highest respect in the Jewish communities.[6]

Jesus' ministry was primarily one of teaching. His followers were called "disciples" or "learners" and spent most of their time receiving instruction from the Master Teacher.

The Gift in the Early Church

As Jesus was ready to ascend into heaven, He left the disciples with this commandment: "Go ye therefore, and *teach* all nations, baptizing them in the name of the Father, and of the Son, and of the Holy Ghost: *teaching* them to observe all things whatsoever I have commanded you" (Matthew 28:19,20). When Jesus said "teach," He used the Greek word *matheteuo,* meaning "to enroll as a scholar, to make to become a pupil." When He said "teaching," in this passage, He used the Greek word *didasko,* meaning "to teach or to instruct."

Jesus gave a twofold commandment. First, the disciples were to preach or evangelize with His gospel (good news). Second, they were to establish doctrine and practices within the spirit and the letter of God's Word (His teachings), and teach or indoctrinate His followers in these truths. Therefore, the apostles were "daily in the temple, and in every house, [where] they ceased not to teach and preach Jesus Christ" (Acts 5:42). "And they continued steadfastly in the apostles' doctrine" (Acts 2:42).

Teaching became one of the most important spiritual gifts in the Early Church. The apostle Paul listed teaching in every one of his major listings of the gifts. (See Romans 12:7; 1 Corinthians 12:28; 14:19; Ephesians 4:11.) Paul himself was a master teacher; some believe he was the greatest teacher aside from Jesus himself. Many of his letters were simply written lessons. Paul said a bishop should be "apt to teach" (1 Timothy 3:2), and instructed Timothy to expand the circle of teachers: "And the things that thou hast heard of me among many witnesses, the same commit thou to faithful men, who shall be able to teach others also" (2 Timothy 2:2).

Ephesians 4:11 says: "And he gave . . . pastors and teachers." The Greek word used here, *didaskalos,* meaning "an instructor," is a form of the Greek word that was used in the Great Commission and was translated "teaching." Whether those in the Early Church were called teachers or instructors, their command was the same: to recruit disciples (followers) of Jesus Christ and cause them to become professed followers of Him.

Their second responsibility was to teach or instruct these followers in His doctrine. A teacher is one who makes others aware of something, imparts knowledge to them, directs them, and trains or accustoms them to some action. An instructor is one who informs, methodically imparts knowledge, or furnishes direction.

The apostle Paul set goals for the teachers in the church at Ephesus. These gifts, he said, had been given "to prepare God's people for works of service, so that the body of Christ may be built up until we all reach unity in the faith and in the knowledge of the Son of God and become mature" (Ephesians 4:12,13, NIV). Consistent instruction in correct doctrine would achieve these goals of unity and maturity.

The Gift in the Contemporary Church

The Great Commission has not changed. The command of Jesus to the apostles is the same to us. We must both evangelize and instruct.

When Paul spoke to the elders of the Ephesian church at Miletus, he outlined three responsibilities which any Sunday school teacher has to his class. As recorded in Acts 20:28-30 these three are: first, to lead the flock as an overseer (v. 28); second, to feed the flock (v. 28); and third, to protect the flock (vv. 29,30).[7]

First, the teacher must lead his Sunday school class, developing his own leadership characteristics. Among these are possessing a positive vision and being committed to and personally involved in seeing that vision become reality. While tradition offers valuable lessons, a leader must be able to allow the creative genius of the Holy Spirit to work within and through him, innovating methods to reach his God-given goals. A leader must communicate his vision, making his vision their goal. Then he must delegate responsibility, drawing from the gifts that God has put in every born-again pupil.

However, a leader cannot be so idealistic that he does not perceive the present position of those he would lead, and be acceptant of their position and tolerant of their initial uncertain responses to his plans.

Most of all, a leader must model by example what he would have his students become, and create opportunities for fellowship with his students in and out of the classroom, so they will have ample opportunity to emulate his example.

Jesus was a model to His disciples. So must we be. Students learn more from what we are than from what we say. So that our pupils can see what we are, we must be with them at times other than during the Sunday school hour. We must make opportunities for pupil-teacher activities.

Jesus' followers were called disciples. Modeling and discipling are closely related. But, whereas modeling is setting an example, discipling is allowing opportunity for that example to be practiced. Therefore, Jesus sent out the Twelve (Luke 9:1,2), and later the Seventy (Luke 10:1), to practice and reinforce what He had taught them. They often failed, but He kept teaching, modeling, and discipling them again.

Second, if the teacher is to feed his flock, he must possess life-giving food. Innovative teaching methods are a necessary ingredient to keep lessons attractive and palatable, but unfortunately, some teachers know more about how to teach than what to teach. A curiosity and thirst to know more of His fullness brings constant study of the Bible and its doctrines.

Not all Christian experiences are pleasant at the time, but with them we can "comfort them which are in any trouble, by the comfort wherewith we ourselves are comforted of God" (2 Corinthians 1:4).

The ability to impart knowledge is one sign of the gift of teaching. A liberal seasoning of inspiration will entice our students to relish our knowledge of His Word. We must help them to apply each lesson to their everyday situations, making God's principles their principles.

The teacher's third major responsibility is to protect the flock. The "bond of peace" referred to in Ephesians 4:3 has been called the "ligament of acceptance," and rightfully so. Ephesians 4:16 reads: "The whole body, joined and held together by every supporting ligament, grows and builds itself up in love, as each part does its work" (NIV).

The ministry of teaching is not to pull apart, but to hold together; not to condemn, but to support. As Abraham interceded for Lot (Genesis 18:23-32), as Moses held back God's wrath against Israel (Numbers 14:11-20), and as Jesus would not allow Satan to sift the apostle Peter as wheat (Luke 22:31,32), we must hold fast to our pupils.

Let Jesus' prayer for His disciples (John 17) be our prayer and practice today. We must hold fast to those He has put in our care! We must refuse to allow our students to slip from God's grace!

Teaching and Revival

Some churches today have deemphasized Sunday school. In many churches, the number who attend Sunday morning worship services exceeds those who attend the education classes. Worship is essential, but it cannot replace the study of God's Word. Jesus declared that we must worship Him "in spirit and in truth" (John 4:24). As we emphasize Acts 2:4, let us also emphasize Acts 2:42.

Some evangelicals have called for the Sunday school's burial. It is interesting to note that many of the objections being voiced are echoes of the criticisms that were hurled against the Sunday school by denominational leaders in the 1950s. Now many leaders of these denominations realize how absolutely essential Christian education is to the church's health and growth.

Lyle Schaller researched the death of hundreds of church congregations. One of the four things that these churches shared was a previous curtailment of their Sunday schools. Sunday school, according to Peter Wagner, has been the greatest church growth device of the past two centuries. Warren Hartman, research analyst of the United Methodist Church, determined from their denominational statistics that there is no significant correlation between worship attendance and church growth, but there is an almost perfect correlation between Sunday school enrollment and membership gain.[8]

Our churches will grow on worship alone, but in a few years we too will pay the price for a lack of education. Sunday school provides small-group fellowship, lay involvement in ministry, a training and proving ground for future church leaders, systematic teaching of the Bible on each individual's level of understanding, and an organization that permits the personal touch and provides a workable system of follow-up.

D. V. Hurst observed that the rise and decline of Israel as a nation paralleled the emphasis that was placed on teaching God's Word. King Jehoshaphat, facing idolatrous influences, trained teachers and sent them throughout Judah to teach the "book of the law of the Lord" (2 Chronicles 17:9). After this knowledge was gained, it could be recorded: "Jehoshaphat waxed great exceedingly" (2 Chronicles 17:12). Renewed interest in the teaching ministry under Ezra and Nehemiah resulted in a revival that was unequaled since Joshua led Israel (Nehemiah 8:17).

Christian education seeks to do more than impart knowledge of truth to the head; it seeks to transform the life, by means of the Holy Spirit and the Word."[9]

Definition of "Ministry"

What is meant by the "ministry" of teaching in the church? The story is told of a church conference speaker who asked his audience to stand. He then asked all of the ministers to remain standing so he could recognize them. Over 90 percent of the congregation sat down.[10] Actually, all of them were ministers, but they thought he wanted only the pastors, evangelists, and missionaries to remain standing. Often we use the word *minister* when we mean "pastor."

Matthew 20:26 says: "But whosoever will be great among you, let him be your minister." *Minister* is translated from the Greek word *diakonos,* from which we derive the English word *deacon.* Here it is used in the verb form and literally means "to be in the act of waiting on or attending."

God has called us and has given us the special gift of pastor-teacher. This grace of God has promoted us to being a servant of the body of Christ. Let us never forget our servant role. Servants have no rights; they are not their own; they are bought with a price (1 Corinthians 6:19,20).

The Teacher and the Total Ministries of the Church

Roy Zuck makes several valid observations concerning the spiritual gift of teaching and its relationship to the entire body of Jesus Christ. First, every believer has some gift, however small or insignificant it may seem, to exercise in the Body (1 Corinthians 12:7,11,27). Second, there is great diversity, yet unity, among the gifts (1 Corinthians 12:28-30). Third, these undeserved gifts are divinely and sovereignly bestowed; therefore, they should be exercised with humility (1 Corinthians 12:11,18). Fourth, God has given these spiritual gifts for the edification, profit, and benefit of the body of Christ, rather than for an outward display of an individual's abilities (1 Corinthians 14:4,5,12,26).[11]

Acts 6 records the appointing of the first deacons. Just as Jethro, Moses' father-in-law, advised Moses to delegate some of his responsibilities (Exodus 18:13-26), so the apostles needed to search out "men of honest report, full of the Holy Ghost and wisdom, whom we may appoint over this *business*" (Acts 6:3). The Greek word here translated "business," literally means "to furnish whatever is needed."

God, in His infinite wisdom, has given gifts to every member of the body of Christ, "severally as he will" (1 Corinthians 12:11), and has "fitly joined [them] together" (Ephesians 4:16), so that every *need* of the Body will be met. Not all are teachers. Not all are preachers. God gifted the apostles especially to be in the "ministry of the word," and others He gifted to "serve tables."

Greatness in Ministry

It is possible for us to be so sensitive to the needs of other members of the body of Christ that we will know what needs to be done and will do it without recruitment or persuasion.

Second Samuel 23 records the story of David and three of his mighty chiefs who were in the cave of Adullam while the Philistines were encamped at Bethlehem: "And David longed, and said, Oh that one would give me drink of the water of the well of Bethlehem, which is by the gate!" (2 Samuel 23:15). He neither ordered nor asked his men to get him a drink of "hometown water." He just "longed" for it. But his men were so sensitive to their leader's desires that "the three mighty men brake through the host of the Philistines, and drew water out of the well of Bethlehem, that was by the gate, and took it, and brought it to David" (2 Samuel 23:16).

The third chapter of 2 Kings gives us another beautiful illustration of this point. The kings of Israel, Judah, and Edom were going to war against the king of Moab. As they passed through the "wilderness of Edom . . . there was no water for the host" (2 Kings 3:8,9). Suddenly, the kings decided to talk to God about this project:

> But Jehoshaphat said, Is there not here a phophet of the Lord, that we may inquire of the Lord by him? And one of the king of Israel's servants answered and said, Here is Elisha the son of Shaphat, *which poured water on the hands of Elijah* (2 Kings 3:11).

What was Elisha's "claim to fame"? It was not that he had divided the Jordan River (2 Kings 2:13,14). It was not that he had healed the waters of Jericho (2 Kings 2:19-22). It was that he had been a servant of a servant of God! Elisha had poured water on the hands of Elijah, when Elisha had been Elijah's disciple. He had served where there was a need!

But wasn't this what Jesus taught when He said: "But whosoever will be great among you, let him be your minister [servant]" (Matthew 20:26)?

Called and Gifted, but Not Used

How sad it is to see Christian men and women divinely called to a specific ministry and supernaturally gifted of God to perform this ministry, but not usable in His kingdom because of an unyielding, unmoldable spirit—a spirit that refuses to accept any authority or leadership.

The psalmist David prayed that God would guard him from such a calamity: "Create in me a clean heart, O God; and renew a right spirit within me. . . . The sacrifices of God are a broken spirit: a broken and a contrite heart, O God, thou wilt not despise" (Psalm 51:10,17).

---

[1]D. V. Hurst, *And He Gave Teachers* (Springfield, MO: Gospel Publishing House, 1955), p. 8.

[2]Judson Cornwall, *Profiles of a Leader* (Plainfield, NJ: Logos International, 1980), p. 25.

[3]Roy B. Zuck, *Spiritual Power in Your Teaching* (Chicago, IL: Moody Press, 1972), p. 69.

[4]*Ibid.*, p. 40.

[5]*Ibid.*, p. 71.

[6]Hurst, *And He Gave Teachers*, pp. 2-7.

[7]Elmer Towns, *The Successful Sunday School and Teachers Guidebook* (Carol Stream, IL: Creation House, 1976), p. 178.

[8]"Trends for the 80s," *Sectional Sunday School Seminar* (Springfield, MO: National Sunday School Dept., 1980), pp. 3,4.

[9]Zuck, *Spiritual Power in Your Teaching*, pp. 63,65.

[10]Cornwall, *Profiles of a Leader*, p. 12.

[11]Zuck, *Spiritual Power in Your Teaching*, pp. 66-69.

2

Commitment to the Ministry of Teaching

> And Jesus said unto him, No man, having put his hand to the plow, and looking back, is fit for the kingdom of God (Luke 9:62).

It was not enough that Jesus was sent to this world to become its Saviour, He had to be committed to His ministry. Satan tempted Jesus with the easy way, saying: "If thou therefore wilt worship me, all shall be thine" (Luke 4:7). Three years later Jesus was still tempted as He prayed, "Take away this cup from me: nevertheless, not what I will, but what thou wilt" (Mark 14:36). But "for the *joy* that was set before him [He] endured the cross, despising the shame, and is set down at the right hand of the throne of God" (Hebrews 12:2).

Called to Commitment

"God acquires His leaders from the *available* ones. God does not have a draft; He depends upon volunteers—persons who make themselves of service to God."[1]

It was one thing for Isaiah to see "the Lord sitting upon a throne, high and lifted up, and his train filled the temple," and then to hear Him say, "Whom shall I send, and who will go for us?" It was yet another thing for Isaiah to answer, "Here am I; send me" (Isaiah 6:1,8). It was one thing for Jesus to say to Simon Peter: "Fear not; from henceforth thou shalt catch men." It was yet another thing for Peter, James, and John to forsake all and follow him (Luke 5:10,11).

Not everyone who is called of God responds in the

affirmative. The rich young ruler "went away sorrowful: for he had great possessions" (Matthew 19:22). As Jesus told the parable of the marriage feast, He said, "Many are called, but few are chosen" (Matthew 22:14), because many "made light of it, and went their ways" (Matthew 22:5). The servant with the one talent was afraid, and went and hid his talent. "His lord answered and said unto him, Thou wicked and slothful servant. . . . Cast ye the unprofitable servant into outer darkness" (Matthew 25:25,26,30). Jesus said: "Every branch in me that beareth not fruit he taketh away" (John 15:2).

These and other verses, such as James 2:20, let us know that it is no small matter with God when He calls us and gives us abilities to use in His kingdom, if we do not act accordingly.

God has called us and gifted us for service in His kingdom. How fortunate we are to be called of God! Yet, how awesome and obligating is the responsibility that comes with the gift.

Motivated to Commitment

Motivation is the energy and direction of our lives. It is the force that causes people to act or not act. Motivation is that force within the individual, rather than without, that incites him to action. Motivation is any need, idea, emotion, or organic state that prompts an action.

Human Motivational Methods

How can we motivate called and gifted members of the body of Jesus Christ to reach their potential in Him? Listed below are eight human motivational methods that have been used:

1. Duress—physical threat.
2. Compulsion—strong verbal appeal.
3. Coercion—largely social pressure from demands of the group.
4. Duty—based on your role; such as, saying you must act a certain way because of who you are or what position you hold.
5. Obligation—an appeal based on responsibility, regardless of your role.

6. Expectation—doing what you or the group expects you to do.

7. Desire—based on the "I want to" principle.

8. Fulfillment—based on knowing what you can do and desiring to achieve that limit.

Of course, we should never use duress, compulsion, or coercion. In fact, we should strive to use only desire and fulfillment.

Spiritual Motivational Methods

Beyond the realms of human influence and forces, we have a source of spiritual motivation. We should strive to be motivated exclusively by these spiritual motives without regard for self-interests or interpersonal and situational forces. These spiritual forces are found in 2 Corinthians 4 and 5:

1. Faith—"We having the same spirit of faith" (4:13).

2. Eternal life—"Knowing that he which raised up the Lord Jesus shall raise up us also . . ." (4:14).

3. Heavenly home—"We have . . . a house not made with hands, eternal in the heavens" (5:1).

4. His acceptance—"We labour, that . . . we may be accepted of him" (5:9).

5. Terror (fear)—"Knowing therefore the terror of the Lord, we persuade men" (5:11).

6. Transformation—"Old things are passed away; behold, all things are become new" (5:17).

7. Commission—"God . . . hath given to us the ministry of reconciliation" (5:18).

Value Structure Determines Motivation

Earlier in this chapter we defined motivation as being "any need, idea, emotion, or organic state that prompts action." Our ideas determine our value structure—what is important to us. Ideas can become so strong that they involve our emotions, so that we are emotional about our values.

It would seem, therefore, that the very seat of commitment

to the ministry of teaching is in our value structure—those things that have become important to us; those things that we love. Jesus prescribed what our value structure should be when He said:

> Thou shalt love the Lord thy God with all thy heart, and with all thy soul, and with all thy mind. This is the first and great commandment. And the second is like unto it, Thou shalt love thy neighbor as thyself (Matthew 22:37-39).

Herein are our two priorities: a love of God and a love of others. These motivate us for a commitment to the ministry of teaching.

A Love of God

Our love of God and of His Son must be our highest priority. We must place the highest possible value on being full of His Holy Spirit if we are to be motivated to fulfill our calling.

On the night Jesus was arrested, the apostle Peter denied his Lord, valuing his personal safety. After Jesus was crucified, had risen from the dead, and had shown himself to His disciples, Peter said, "I go a fishing" (John 21:3). Morning dawned over a fishing boat that still contained no fish, but Jesus was faithful to those whom He had called even in this day of disappointment. He commanded that they "cast the net on the right side of the ship. . . . They cast therefore, and now they were not able to draw it for the multitude of fishes" (John 21:6).

After they had brought their 153 fish to shore and had eaten the breakfast prepared by Jesus, He confronted Peter with a question regarding his values. "Jesus saith to Simon Peter . . . lovest thou me more than these?" (John 21:15). "What are you really sold out to, Peter? These fish, nets, and boats? other fishermen? Or are you sold out to Me and My calling?"

Peter replied, "Yea, Lord; thou knowest that I love thee. [Jesus] saith unto him, Feed my lambs" (John 21:15). Twice

Jesus repeated His question. Twice Peter repeated his answer. Twice Jesus repeated His instructions.

> God picks His leaders from those who are willing and able to disentangle themselves from the affairs of this life. . . . But perhaps the greatest facet of availability that God looks for is a heart that cries out after God.[2]

Love of God or Love of Things?

A. W. Tozer wrote:

> Our woes began when God was forced out of His central shrine and "things" were allowed to enter. Within the human heart "things" have taken over. Men have now by nature no peace within their hearts, for God is crowned there no longer.[3]

God promised Abraham: "I will make thy seed as the dust of the earth: so that if a man can number the dust of the earth, then shall thy seed also be numbered" (Genesis 13:16). Yet when he was 100 years old and his wife Sarah was 90, they still had not had their child (Genesis 17:17). But, at the promise of God, Isaac was born (Genesis 21:5).

Later God said to Abraham, "Take now thy son, thine only son Isaac, whom thou lovest, and get thee into the land of Moriah; and offer him there for a burnt offering" (Genesis 22:2). This child of their old age surely had become the object of their affections. He was the embodiment of God's promise: "In thee shall all families of the earth be blessed" (Genesis 12:3).

Yet in total obedience to God's command, "Abraham rose up early in the morning" and began the 3-day northward journey. As "Abraham stretched forth his hand, and took the knife to slay his son," an angel of the Lord said, "Lay not thine hand upon the lad, neither do thou any thing unto him: *for now I know that thou fearest God,* seeing thou hast not withheld thy son, thine only son, from me" (Genesis 22:10,12). Who was central in Abraham's heart, Isaac or God?

Now Abraham had everything—sheep, camels, a wife, Isaac, friends—but he *possessed nothing.* Abraham had become as Jesus later would teach: "Blessed are the poor in spirit: for theirs is the kingdom of heaven" (Matthew 5:3). Jesus said unto His disciples: "If any man will come after me, let him deny himself, and take up his cross, and follow me" (Matthew 16:24).

Love of Others

Our second major love or value must be a love of others.

> A love for the pupil enables the teacher to aim at the pupil's heart and in so doing to draw from his heart a similar response, and to turn that love ultimately to God. Love is the supreme motive for all Christian work and especially that of the teacher.[4]

We are nearing the beginning of the third generation since large numbers of wives and mothers found their way into the workers' marketplace during World War II. We are well into the second generation of TV kids. Mothers who work during a child's early years obviously do not have as much time to render the quantity of love, time, and attention to their offspring as do mothers who do not work outside of the home. In almost all homes television has become either a substitute parent or at least an influence of major proportions.

These two factors alone have dehumanized our relationships in the last 30 to 40 years at an ever accelerating rate. Our society is filled with those who actually do not know how to love. They can neither give nor respond to love, because they have never experienced it.

As with declining civilizations of old, love has become worthless and life empty. People are becoming detached from those around them; moving toward a robotlike existence. Young people today are taught not to make too large of an investment in love or friendships and to avoid excessive dependence on others. "Live life for today!" "If it doesn't work, throw it away!"

Paul foretold these end times when he wrote: "There will be terrible times in the last days. People will be . . . without love" (2 Timothy 3:1-3, NIV). It is into this society that we must carry God's message of love. Nothing but our long-suffering patience and His transforming power can reverse generations of lovelessness.

Methods of Motivation in the Contemporary Church

Despite our love of God and others, we occasionally become discouraged and need remotivating to fulfill the tasks in the ministry of teaching. Motivation begins with recruitment, is aided by initial training and continuing education, and is crowned with appreciation for a job well done.

Recruitment

Recruitment should begin with a scheduled visit between the pastor and/or Sunday school leadership and the prospective teacher. A prepared job description should be used to keep the conversation focused on the opportunities and responsibilities of teaching. No decision should be expected during the initial interview; rather, a time should be scheduled for the prospective teacher to visit the department he is considering. Then time should be allowed for him to seek God's direction before making a decision.

Workers usually perform near the level of their leaders' expectations. When the recruiting "interview" is conducted in a church hallway or by telephone under last-ditch, emergency circumstances, teacher motivation will begin low and decline.

Recruitment may be easier if the initial assignment is to be a "teacher assistant" rather than having the full responsibility for a class. In addition, time is allowed each new worker to search out his calling during this period of discipling by a master teacher.

Training

While this period of apprenticeship makes recruitment

easier, it also has the possibilities of beginning an effective teacher training program. As we will discuss in the next chapter, every teacher should complete the four *Fundamentals for Sunday School Workers* books and one of the age-level handbooks available from Gospel Publishing House as a foundational study.

Beyond this, regular Sunday school staff meetings offer several elements of continuing education and motivation:[5]

1. *Fellowship.* An open time at the beginning of each staff meeting allows teachers opportunity to fellowship and share ideas that work.

2. *Worship.* Staff worship opens communication to our ultimate Source of encouragement and instruction.

3. *Information.* The Sunday school leadership should present a workshop containing usable information rather than a rehashing of age-old slogans or problems. Each month's Leaders Edition of the *Sunday School Counselor* contains a "Workers Conference" column. Gospel Publishing House or your local Christian bookstore can provide additional materials.

4. *Application.* Never present facts without allowing time for practice in their practical application.

5. *Breakaway.* A good staff meeting allows time for departmental group meetings in which additional specific information can be shared and made applicable.

6. *Prayer.* A concluding time of earnest prayer for each other applies a balm to spirits that are sore from serving.

Leadership does not have the sole responsibility for continuing training and motivation. Jude 20 says: "But ye, beloved, building up *yourselves.*" And Galatians 6:2 admonishes: "Bear ye one *another's* burdens." Fellowship and prayers begun at Sunday school staff meetings should continue afterward. While another teacher is visiting in your home, you may find a simple solution to a nagging classroom problem. When you are on vacation, visit the Christian education departments of other churches to gain new and workable ideas.

Make use of your Sunday school's library of workers training books, other informational and inspirational books, magazines, and audio or audiovisual cassettes. If no such library exists, start one by buying a book, reading it, and then making it available to other workers on your staff.

Usually not enough sources of motivation and continuing education can be found within the resources of any one church. Take advantage of annual Sunday school conventions. Most sectional and district Christian education departments conduct periodic seminars which both inform and inspire.

Appreciation and Recognition

Even though most Sunday school teachers are ministering solely because of their love of their Lord and their pupils, sometimes even the most consecrated and well-trained teacher becomes discouraged. A lack of appreciation and recognition is often the culprit.

An annual teacher-appreciation banquet is the least that can be done. An annual Teacher Appreciation Sunday gives teachers who are often in the corner of the church basement visibility before the entire church body. Such a service can also aid the teacher recruitment process.

Just as the responsibility for training is not solely that of the leadership, neither are appreciation and recognition. Take every opportunity to express appreciation to each other. Send birthday cards, flowers, or personally written letters on birthdays and wedding anniversaries. A note of appreciation on a "no special occasion day" is such an encouragement to sagging spirits! Other anniversaries that can be remembered are the date a staff member began teaching (if anyone remembers!), and the date an initial teacher training course was completed. Remember both those who are ill or sorrowing and those who are rejoicing over some important event. The Sunday school may wish to appoint a corresponding secretary to write such recognitions, but remember to do your part too!

Sometimes teachers become discouraged because they are in

the wrong area of ministry. Someone who would work well with teenagers may be a "nervous wreck" with preschool children, and vice versa. If you are dissatisfied with your assignment, request a change. When the annual teacher evaluation is done (which we will discuss in chapter 9), it would be advisable to ask each teacher if he feels comfortable in his present assignment.

Personality clashes are not unknown among teachers. When all else fails, gracefully request a transfer to a new ministry within the Sunday school.

When teachers learn innovative methods of teaching, they can become discouraged with their facilities, available equipment, or materials. Try making improvements that cost little while working toward the ideal. Set a plan and target date for reaching the optimum.

Satisfied teachers are a good advertisement to attract both students and workers. Investments in proper recruitment, training, and recognition pay big dividends!

Sticking With the Job

> Unfortunately, not all available persons have the stick-to-itiveness that is required to be a leader of God. . . . God does not hire by the hour; He contracts for life. Once God's commission is accepted there is no decommissioning.[6]

Luke 14:28-35 contains three parables concerning counting the costs and staying with the job once we are committed to it. (Please read these verses.) We must be committed to our ministries of teaching in such a way that we can approach our Heavenly Father at life's end, saying, as Jesus did: "I have glorified thee on the earth: I have finished the work which thou gavest me to do" (John 17:4).

---

[1]Judson Cornwall, *Profiles of a Leader* (Plainfield, NJ: Logos International, 1980), p. 11.

[2]*Ibid.*, pp. 12,13.

[3]A. W. Tozer, *The Pursuit of God* (Harrisburg, PA: Christian Publications, Inc., 1948), pp. 21,22.

[4]D. V. Hurst, *And He Gave Teachers* (Springfield, MO: Gospel Publishing House, 1955), pp. 34,35.

[5]Elmer Towns, *The Successful Sunday School and Teachers Guidebook* (Carol Stream, IL: Creation House, 1976), p. 190.

[6]Cornwall, *Profiles of a Leader,* pp. 11,12.

3

Preparation for the Ministry of Teaching

> And Jesus increased in wisdom and stature, and in favor with God and man (Luke 2:52).

It was not enough that Jesus was sent to this earth and He was committed to doing His Father's will. Even He *prepared* for the ministry that was before Him, and throughout His ministry on earth, He continued to be properly prepared.

Why did Jesus wait until he was 30 years old to begin His earthly ministry? Why didn't the apostle Paul begin his ministry of preaching immediately upon his conversion (Galatians 1:15-19)?

Luke 2:41-52 gives us insight into Jesus' early preparations. (Please pause long enough from your reading of this text to study these verses.) Luke 2:52 acts as our outline to this chapter: "And Jesus increased in *wisdom* and *stature,* and *in favor with God* and *[in favor with] man.*"

Wisdom

It is easy to take comfort in such Scripture passages as 1 Corinthians 1:26: "For ye see your calling, brethren, how that not many wise men *after the flesh,* not many mighty, not many noble, are called." But James 1:5 reads: "If any of you lack wisdom, let him ask of God, that giveth to all men liberally, and upbraideth not; and it shall be given him." God puts no premium on ignorance. Rather, He puts a premium on God-given wisdom that remains subject to His bidding.

Jesus spent much of His preparation years in Scripture

study. He was "in the temple, sitting in the midst of the doctors, both hearing them, and asking them questions" (Luke 2:46). In Jesus' 40 days of fasting He was repeatedly tempted by the devil. But every temptation was overcome with "It is written" (Luke 4:4,8,12). Those years of study paid off! So many people today succumb to temptations and false doctrines because they are ignorant of the Scriptures: "My people are destroyed for lack of knowledge" (Hosea 4:6).

One would think that Sunday school teachers would certainly know the Bible. Yet in a recent survey of over 1,200 Sunday school teachers from over 100 churches of varying sizes, a shocking 75 percent failed a 25-question multiple choice test on Bible knowledge! A similar test on the doctrines of the Assemblies of God was failed by 71 percent of these teachers. In this same survey, 57 percent could not pass the test on methods of teaching, and 52 percent did not adequately understand the Sunday school system.

To help alleviate this problem, the national Sunday School Department has developed a vital teacher certification program designed to build strong Sunday schools through qualified, efficient teachers. To earn the certification award a Sunday school worker must initially do these two things:

1. Complete the four units of the *Fundamentals for Sunday School Workers* (FSSW) training course.
2. Read the appropriate age-level or administration handbook.

The titles of the four FSSW books are: (1)*Your Sunday School at Work,* (2)*Knowing Your Bible,* (3)*Understanding Our Doctrine,* and (4)*Mastering the Methods.* Each of these books is available from Gospel Publishing House in both student and instructor editions. An instructor's packet of overhead transparencies aids the learning process.

Each book contains 13 lessons, making it a convenient adult Sunday school elective course for those who are planning to become teachers and for those veteran teachers who need a refresher study. Other churches have found the hour before the Sunday evening service or a midweek Bible study night to be an opportune time to teach these books, particularly *Knowing Your Bible* and *Understanding Our Doctrine.* The courses may be taught in the local church by the pastor, the minister of Christian education, the Sunday school superintendent, a public school teacher or administrator, or any other person the pastor feels is qualified for this assignment.

The second requirement in the initial phase of teacher certification is to read the appropriate age-level or administration handbook. The preschool, elementary, youth, and adult handbooks emphasize creative classroom methodology. The administration handbook surveys the principles of Sunday school leadership, organization, and administration. Each of these five handbooks is available from Gospel Publishing House. The entire certification study is now available through the Berean School of the Bible, the correspondence school of the Assemblies of God in Springfield, Missouri.

Certification status can be maintained with the annual refresher study or by individual study. The church-sponsored refresher study can center on the annual workers training book-of-the-year, such as this book.

Finally, good tools are a must for an effective worker. A study Bible, a *complete* concordance, Bible maps, a Bible dictionary, a book on Bible customs, etc., allow a teacher to minister more effectively and efficiently. Magazines are a way to remain current between annual books and seminars. The *Sunday School Counselor* from Gospel Publishing House is a must for every Assemblies of God Sunday school worker.

Stature

"And Jesus increased in . . . stature" (Luke 2:52).

> What! know ye not that your body is the temple of the Holy Ghost which is in you, which ye have of God, and ye are not your own? For ye are bought with a price: therefore glorify God in your body, and in your spirit, which are God's (1 Corinthians 6:19,20).

The Scriptures make it perfectly clear that we are to care for our body and its health if we are to minister effectively. Good health is basically a matter of *using* good common sense.

Many of our health problems are not organically but behaviorally originated. We learn behavior patterns from our parents in such subtle ways that we are often unaware of them. Patterns of eating, sleeping, working, exercising, etc., were learned to some degree almost before we could walk or talk. We can either accept those behavioral patterns as our own or try by the help of God to change them. Just as He can take away the craving for tobacco or alcohol, He can take away an ungodly appetite for food or a bent toward workaholism or stress. Losing weight is only half the battle. We have not won the war until we keep the weight off. Most diets fail in the long run because they ask us to give up things we like. Common sense tells us that when we go back to old eating patterns, we will soon return to our old weight. We must cut down, not out.

We must learn not to eat except at mealtime and except while seated at a dining table. And we must also rethink our food-oriented Christian fellowship. Surely we can be friendly without eating all the time!

Physical activity need not be strenuous. Walking is undoubtedly one of the most beneficial exercises; however, it needs to be brisk enough to raise the pulse rate. Moderate physical activity with no breaks for half an hour is vastly superior to much more strenuous exercise with even brief pauses. For one thing, plaques of fat, which can eventually cause strokes and heart attacks, can be cleared from the arteries through an uninterrupted, accelerated pulsing of blood through them.[1]

Too much food and a lack of physical activity are the two primary hindrances to American health, but there are other factors. Drugs have become epidemic. Not only illegal drugs, but also legal ones can be harmful if taken unwisely. Very few drink enough water, while most of us consume too much Coke, tea, and coffee. Other health-affecting factors are our general disposition, home environment, job satisfaction, driving habits, home location, and marital status.

In Favor With God

"And Jesus increased . . . in favor with God" (Luke 2:52). Jesus' desire to know the Father and His will never ceased during His earthly ministry. The night before His crucifixion, Jesus earnestly sought the Father's will as He prayed in Gethsemane: "Father, if thou be willing, remove this cup from me: nevertheless, not my will, but thine, be done. . . . And being in an agony he prayed more earnestly . . ." (Luke 22:42,44).

Perhaps one of the greatest weaknesses of some of today's Sunday school teachers is that they are no longer growing in their relationship with God; they have ceased to know God better.

Luke 10:38-42 relates the story of Jesus' visit to Martha's house. While Martha "was cumbered about much serving," her sister Mary "sat at Jesus' feet, and heard his word." Martha complained to Jesus, "Lord, dost thou not care that my sister hath left me to serve alone? bid her therefore that she help me." Jesus' reply was a pronouncement of priorities not only to Mary and Martha, but also to us today: "Martha, Martha, thou art careful and troubled about many things: but one thing is needful; and Mary hath chosen that good part, which shall not be taken away from her."

The good part! Sitting at Jesus' feet and hearing His words! Oh, God, help us to set proper priorities! Let us cry as did the Psalmist of old: "As the hart panteth after the water brooks, so panteth my soul after thee, O God" (Psalm 42:1).

Again we call your attention to A. W. Tozer's little book *The Pursuit of God,* where we find these words in chapter IV, "Apprehending God":

> To most people God is an inference, not a reality. He is a deduction from evidence which they consider adequate; but He remains personally unknown to the individual.

> "He *must* be," they say, "therefore we believe He is." . . . The possibility of intimate acquaintance with Him has not entered their minds. [2]

If ever there was a prophet of Old Testament days who could claim knowledge of God, it would have been Moses. How easy it would have been for Moses to boastfully say, "I know God, I've been in His very midst. I've talked to Him as a friend." (See Exodus 19:20; 33:11.) But no, that was not Moses' attitude. In fact, after all these experiences he said to God, ". . . Show me now thy way, that I may know thee" (Exodus 33:13). Surely it was because of this hunger to be in favor with God that the psalmist David could pen: "He made known his *ways* unto Moses, his *acts* unto the children of Israel" (Psalm 103:7).

As with Moses, how easy it would have been for Paul to boastfully say, "I know God. I've been to the third heaven. I've heard words which cannot be uttered." (See 2 Corinthians 12:2-4). But no, that was not Paul's attitude either. Instead, he cried, ". . . that I may *know him*" (Philippians 3:10)! Oh, God, give us teachers with that same thirst for You!

Dr. C. M. Ward learned during his days as a student that there is no substitute for knowing God. He relates this turning point in *The C. M. Ward Story*:

> Now I had reached a marvelous point, I had been melted. . . . Suddenly my life moved into proper orbit. I saw that my target was *to know Him*. . . . I decided to get better acquainted with Jesus.[3]

You may ask, "How can I know God better?" Well, how do you get to know anyone better? Yes, you spend time with that person. You talk. You listen. You read what you have written to each other.

The first psalm gives us timely advice:

> Blessed is the man that walketh not in the counsel of the ungodly, nor standeth in the way of sinners, nor sitteth in the seat of the scornful. But his delight is in the

> law of the Lord; and in his law doth he *meditate* day and night (Psalm 1:1,2).

How sad to see Christian people never discussing the riches and goodness of God! Of course, this is not to say that we cannot take time for conversations about the things of this life. But there is danger lurking for Christians who never have time to discuss God with others. There is even a greater danger in the lives of Christians who never have time to discuss God with God.

Despite the illicit sex, violence, and crime that television depicts, and the influence it has in altering value structures, the most damaging aspect of television is the time it takes. Ask yourself: "What am I *not* doing when I am watching television?" Well, I am not communicating with my spouse. I am not spending quality time with my children. I am not visiting with my friends. I am not visiting my Sunday school students. I am not making improvements on our home. I am not taking a course at the nearby junior college. I am not exercising my body. I am not reading my Bible. I am not praying.

Let us pray with A. W. Tozer:

> O God, I have tasted Thy goodness, and it has both satisfied me and made me thirsty for more. I am painfully conscious of my need of further grace. I am ashamed of my lack of desire. . . . Show me Thy glory, I pray Thee, that so I may know Thee indeed.[4]

In Favor With Man

"And Jesus increased in . . . favor with . . . man" (Luke 2:52). How interesting that we see these same elements in the lives of so many other men of Holy Writ. (For example: Jacob [Genesis 32:28], Solomon [2 Chronicles 1:12], Samuel [1 Samuel 2:26], and John the Baptist [Luke 1:80].)

A Pharisee came to Jesus, asking, "Master, which is the great commandment in the law? Jesus said unto him, Thou shalt love the Lord thy God with all thy heart, and with all thy soul, and with all thy mind. This is the first and great commandment. And the second is like unto it, Thou shalt love thy neighbor as thyself. On these two commandments hang all the law and the prophets" (Matthew 22:36-40).

We have already discussed the first part: "Thou shalt love the Lord thy God." Now let us examine the other two elements in this verse: (1)love thy neighbor, and (2)love thyself.

"And Was Subject Unto Them"

The outline for this chapter has been Luke 2:52. A key to Jesus' human relationships is found in the preceding verse: "And he went down with them, and came to Nazareth, and was *subject* unto them" (Luke 2:51).

We too must be about the Father's business, "but if any provide not for his own, and specially for those of his own house, he hath denied the faith, and is worse than an infidel" (1 Timothy 5:8). To "provide" for a family involves more than just money. It also requires quality time, physical contact, emotional support, and spiritual discipling. Ephesians 6:4 instructs: "And, ye fathers, provoke not your children to wrath: but bring them up in the nurture and admonition of the Lord."

Dr. James Dobson produced a series of seven films, titled *Focus on the Family.* In the third film, *Christian Fathering,* he makes these three statements:

> All over this country little children are reaching for fathers who aren't there. . . . I want to evangelize as many people as possible, but my number one job is to evangelize my children. . . . If America is going to survive, it will be because husbands and fathers begin to put their families at the highest level of priorities and reserve something of their time, effort, and energy for leadership within their own homes.[5]

As we learn about God by spending time with Him, so we learn about our families by spending time with them. Yes, we want those who have been called to work in our Sunday schools to be committed to their calling, but our families are our first calling. We need not sacrifice one for the other. It is very possible to involve our families in our teaching ministry. Of course, if our children help us with our interests, it is only fair that we spend time with them in their interests.

Not only was Jesus under the authority of His earthly family, but He was also subject to His earthly government (Matthew 17:24-27; 22:21).

> Let every soul be subject unto the higher powers. For there is no power but of God: the powers that be are ordained of God. Whosoever therefore resisteth the power, resisteth the ordinance of God (Romans 13:1,2).

Please pause long enough in your reading of this text to study both Romans 13:1-8 and 1 Timothy 2:1,2. Especially note Romans 13:8. It is a verse that is often quoted out of context.

"Thou Shalt Love Thy Neighbor as Thyself"

The primary reason that many people do not love their neighbors is because they do not love themselves. Unless we have a healthy self-respect, it is difficult, if not impossible, to love our neighbors.

Low self-esteem cannot be corrected overnight. After all, our self-image has been in the making since we were born. Early in life we were labeled by our parents, siblings, playmates, and teachers. Soon we believed what we were being told about ourselves. But as surely as God can transform us from a life of overt sin, He can cleanse our innermost thoughts, and that includes our self-image. "Be ye transformed by the renewing of your mind" (Romans 12:2).

Here are a few practical suggestions to help you improve your self-esteem:[6]

1. Dress and look your best at all times.
2. Smile.
3. Look people in the eyes.

4. Volunteer your own name first whenever you meet someone new.

5. Respond with a simple, courteous "thank you" when anyone pays you a compliment.

6. Write down what your blessings are, and who and what you are thankful for.

7. When you talk use encouraging, affirmative language. Everything you say about yourself is being recorded by your own self-image.

8. Accept yourself as you are right now, but keep an ongoing self-development plan.

Jesus found it necessary to prepare for His ministry on this earth and to continue preparing for each day's ministry. How much more must we do the same to fulfill our awesome calling in the ministry of teaching. "And Jesus increased in wisdom and stature, and in favor with God and man" (Luke 2:52).

---

[1]Paul Neimark, "It's Earlier Than You Think," *Success,* January 1982, pp. 20-22,56.

[2]A. W. Tozer, *The Pursuit of God* (Harrisburg, PA: Christian Publications, Inc., 1948), pp. 49,50.

[3]Douglas Wead, *The C. M. Ward Story* (Harrison, AR: New Leaf Press, 1976), p. 27.

[4]Tozer, *The Pursuit of God,* p. 20.

[5]Dr. James Dobson, *Christian Fathering* (Waco, TX: Word, Inc., 1979).

[6]Dennis Waitley, "Self-esteem," *Success,* December 1981, p. 51.

4

Understanding the Pupil's Characteristic Needs

I am the good shepherd, and know my sheep, and am known of mine (John 10:14).

To be an effective Sunday school teacher, it is necessary to understand the pupils with whom we work. Age largely determines characteristics; however, not every pupil will display each characteristic or exhibit every need. Our goal is to affect our students' lives for God and eternity in a positive manner. However, it is impossible to accomplish this without an understanding of the physical, mental, social, and emotional characteristics that affect their spiritual development.

Early Childhood

Birth to Two Years

Often the Sunday school teacher is the first nonfamily person to influence a baby's life. The patient, responsive, caring teacher communicates God's love to him with a warm voice and gentle gestures. Young children learn through their senses. The wise teacher provides numerous opportunities for them to touch, hear, see, smell, and taste. Recently the Gospel Publishing House has developed a new curriculum series to use in teaching the child from 6 months to 2 years of age.

Nursery (Two and Three Years)

Physical characteristics. The larger child should not be expected to do more than his smaller friend. Since only the large muscles are developing, handwork should be simple, using large crayons for coloring one object on a piece of paper. Twos and threes have trouble doing more than one thing at a time, so you may find yourself singing a solo while your pupils are busy concentrating on doing the actions.

Mental characteristics. Because the child's group attention span is so short (about 2 to 4½ minutes) all activities should be short—short stories, short songs, short prayers, and short worship times. Repetition is very valuable, since his memory is undependable. The 2- and 3-year-old has difficulty distinguishing between fact and fancy; a fairy tale is as real to him as a true story. Since he does not understand symbolism, it is best not to sing songs like "The Devil Is a Sly Old Fox." Stories from the Old Testament about wars and wicked kings should be avoided. The nursery child learns best by imitating good examples provided by those who teach him. He learns the position and attitude of prayer by watching his teacher; he learns more about kindness and thoughtfulness from example than by what he is told.

Social characteristics. The 2- and 3-year-old enjoys playing by himself. Parallel play is common—each child making his own sand castle rather than all the children working together on the same castle.

Emotional characteristics. The nursery child may be easily upset as he leaves the familiar surroundings of his home and is introduced to the larger environment of the Sunday school. The increased activities of many children may be disquieting, since he has a sensitive nervous system.

Spiritual characteristics. The nursery child has both abilities and limitations in understanding spiritual truth. He enjoys hearing about Jesus' birth and childhood. He knows that Jesus wants to be his friend, that he can talk to God, and that God loves him. He understands that the Bible is God's Word, as he sees his teacher handling it with love and respect.

Beginner (Four and Five Years)

Physical characteristics. The beginner child's large muscles are still developing. Because he does not yet have control of his finer muscles, his handwork should be limited to that which can be easily performed. Sometimes he will break a crayon because of poor muscle coordination. The beginner child has an abundance of energy and wants to be involved in physical activity. It is best to alternate quiet times with periods of activity. He will squirm and wiggle if he is unable to change activities often. His group attention span is only about 5 minutes.

Mental characteristics. Language is a tool the beginner child uses constantly. He now understands 1500 to 2300 words, but uses only about one-third of them. He can more easily give his attention to *doing* rather than *talking* or *listening.* He can memorize a Scripture verse word for word and yet not really understand its meaning. It is better that a child know the meaning of a few short phrases rather than many long verses by rote.

Social characteristics. The beginner child is still self-centered, but he is realizing that others have rights and privileges too. The idea of taking turns is an adjustment in his thinking, but he is helped if his teacher divides his class into small groups so that his turn comes often. The pupil enjoys playing with a group, and feels left out if he is not accepted. He wants the approval of adults more than that of children.

Emotional characteristics. Fear is the outstanding emotion at this age, so the emphasis should be on God's love and care, developing a sense of security.

Spiritual characteristics. Since the beginner child thinks of God as a person, he should be helped to understand that he doesn't need to wait until he is in Sunday school with his head bowed, hands folded, and eyes closed to talk to God.

Children in the early childhood department need the *positive* male model that Christian men provide. Early exposure to men in Sunday school allows children to understand that church is for the entire family, not just for women and children. This need is emphasized with today's increase of single-parent families. Men who are beginning to work in this department may be more comfortable fulfilling the duties of teaching assistants or aides.

Elementary

Included in this department are those children ages 6 through 11. Usually they are divided into three groups: primaries (first and second graders), middlers (third and fourth graders), and juniors (fifth and sixth graders).

Physical characteristics. Because the younger elementary child is still growing at a rapid but uneven pace, he tends to tire easily. Alternate periods of activity with quiet times. The smaller muscles are developing and should be exercised, but during short periods that avoid projects with much detail.

For the older elementary child, this is one of the healthiest periods of his life. Growth is not rapid, and most childhood diseases have come and gone. Consequently, regular attendance can be expected if the activities are exciting.

Mental characteristics. There is a wide range of reading ability in this group, since the younger elementary child is just beginning to recognize written symbols while the older ones have been reading for several years. The younger child's memory is good, allowing him to memorize Scripture verses, even though he may not fully comprehend their meaning.

Since the older elementary pupil is a hero worshiper, now is an excellent time to introduce the Old Testament spiritual giants. He is interested in science and greatly appreciates a teacher who accompanies the group on hikes and shows no distaste for bugs, worms, or frogs. Now, more than at any other time in his life, the elementary pupil can easily memorize and retain facts. This time should be used wisely to commit Scripture verses to memory.

Social characteristics. The younger child enjoys playing with others in groups. Thinking of himself as grown up, he appreciates his teacher not using the term *little*. He still tends to be selfish, because his world has not broadened to any degree; however, the wise teacher can show him how to be thoughtful of others. He respects authority and is very anxious to please his teacher.

The older elementary child is more independent in his thinking and able to accept responsibility. He enjoys doing things for other people. Although he wants to be independent of adults, he depends on the companionship of his peer group of the same sex.

Emotional characteristics. The teacher needs to maintain a calm atmosphere in the classroom, since the younger elementary child is easily excited. It is not unusual for the child to become impatient with himself when he doesn't know all the answers, because he is very conscientious.

The older child of this group is practically fearless, but a great worrier. He is rather hard on himself and becomes upset by his own mistakes. He is learning to control his emotions, and he usually has a good sense of humor.

Spiritual characteristics. Because the younger child enjoys Sunday school so much, he will measure time by Sundays. Since he considers religion to be a natural part of his life, it is easy for him to develop a personal relationship with God. He feels as comfortable talking with Him as with his best friend. This is the time to nourish faith.

Statistics show that more persons accept Christ as their personal Saviour at ages 8 through 11 than at any other time in life. The elementary child has little difficulty believing in the supernatural. The teacher should earnestly pray that each pupil will accept Christ before leaving this department. This older elementary pupil approaches his religion without emotion; he simply wants the facts. It is important for him to understand how Christianity affects his life.

Junior High (Twelve to Fourteen Years)

Physical characteristics. Except for the first 3 years of a child's life, this is the time of the greatest physical growth. Most girls are taller and heavier than the boys. Because of rapid bone and muscular development, the young person needs recreational activities. He needs an understanding teacher who realizes that he does not purposely run into the chairs when he walks into the classroom; he is simply awkward. Times of excess energy alternate with periods of extreme fatigue.

Mental characteristics. Even though the junior high pupil is capable of memorizing, he must have a reason or a use for learning. He reads much—probably more than at any other time in his life—however, he is not discriminating in what he reads. He needs guidance in selecting good materials. He can be challenged to think for himself, using the Scriptures to find solutions to his everyday problems. Sometimes his thinking is quite mature, but at other times it is very childlike.

Social characteristics. The junior high pupil desires so much to be grown up that it is quite devastating for him to be put in a class with juniors. Even if your Sunday school has only three or four junior high pupils, it is much better to allow them to have their own class. Otherwise, they may eventually drop out, unless they are forced by their parents to continue attending. Providing a special class where their needs are met will encourage them to ask others to join. The Sunday school should follow the system of classifying pupils that is used in the community's public schools. For example, a ninth-grader who attends a high school would not relish being in the junior high department at Sunday school, and vice versa. The junior high pupil experiences extreme self-consciousness. For the first time he sees himself as a person; one who is different from others in many ways.

Emotional characteristics. The junior high pupil often feels that he is misunderstood. At times he doesn't even understand himself. His emotions fluctuate, and he seems to have lost the control that he had a couple of years earlier. The teacher should be careful not to build the emotions of his class to a high pitch without providing an outlet for action.

Spiritual characteristics. The junior high pupil is interested in a practical religion—one that is life-changing. Because he now sees himself as an individual, he feels more responsible than ever for his conduct and his future. He understands his need for a Saviour—One who can help him control his conduct. Although he still possesses an element of childlike faith, this is the time when doubts begin to surface; he may even doubt his own salvation. Rather than reprimanding him for these questions, the wise teacher should patiently direct him to God's Word for answers.

Senior High (Fifteen to Seventeen Years)

Physical characteristics. During this period the finer muscles develop, allowing the young person to lose his awkwardness. He now possesses a grown-up, attractive appearance. Physical habits are forming for the rest of life; the Sunday school teacher can guide him into *good* habits. Good physical habits go hand in hand with the development of good spiritual habits. The unhealthy person has difficulty comprehending the things of God.

Mental characteristics. The intellectual powers of the high school student are exercised to their maximum. His memory span is greatly expanded, as ideas rather than words are stored. He is anxious to see logic in everything, and he has learned to control his active imagination.

> Adolescence brings with it a whole new range of intellectual processes that were not previously possible. Most children think concretely. Adolescents can think propositionally. Principles of law and morality are now more readily understood and handled.[1]

Social characteristics. The high school student enjoys opportunities of becoming acquainted with members of the opposite sex. Getting along well with others allows him to develop a feeling of security. One of his greatest needs is being accepted by his peer group. The understanding teacher remembers that the high school pupil wants to organize and lead his own activities.

Emotional characteristics. The high school student expresses all his feelings—love, hate, sorrow, joy, and shame—with intensity. Even though he may appear grown up physically, his emotions are unstable at times. However, by age 16 or 17 he is able to control his emotions in public. The Sunday school teacher should be a dependable counselor with whom inner conflicts can be confided.

Spiritual characteristics. The high school student is interested in a religion that is more than just ideology. He needs a religion of action that will help him make vocational and social choices. Doubts may surface, particularly if his honest questions during his junior high school days were not answered. For the first time in his life he can appreciate the abstract and can understand symbolism.

Adults

Until recently, children held the spotlight in our Sunday schools. We had many more children than adults—as measured by the percentage of the total U.S. population in each age-group. Children also seemed to be more diverse and rapidly changing; requiring more understanding and teaching skills on the part of the teacher.

Today the tables have turned. For the first time in United States history there are more adults than children in our population, and studies indicate this trend will continue. The World War II baby-boom "bubble" is now moving through our middle adult population. Between 1980 and 1990, the number of adults aged 30-39 will increase over 28 percent, those aged 40-49 will increase over 37 percent, but those aged 20-29 will *decrease* about 4 percent. Should our Lord tarry until the year 2,000, those over age 65 will constitute nearly one-third of our population.

In times past, adults were thought to be homogeneous; experiencing only gradual change. Either this was never true or it is no longer. As adults diversify and change, so do their needs. The Word of God offers ultimate answers, but it must be applied to people's real needs as opposed to traditional ones. Just as we would never consider having one big "children's class," neither can one sweeping "adults' class" minister to such diversity.

Single Adults

Recent statistics indicate that there are over 50 million single adults in the United States. Traditionally, the church has been marriage- and family-oriented, but singles now constitute too large a segment of our society to be overlooked. In the past, singles often have been left out and misunderstood. Sometimes they have even been considered a threat to married people.

Singles have many of the same problems as married people—finances, establishing a home, transportation, raising children, etc. They too suffer from shattered dreams, damaged egos, and a low self-image; however, they must face these problems alone. We all need fellowship, acceptance, a sense of belonging, consideration, and companionship. In particular, some singles need help dealing with alienation, loss, and rejection.

Fifty percent of the single population have never married because of schooling, career pursuits and other obligations, handicaps, enjoying the freedom of singleness, or because they have never met someone with whom they want to spend the rest of their lives. Half the marriages in this country end in divorce. Sixty-five percent of all married women are widowed by age 60; by age 80, 80 percent are widows. Each of these groups of singles has unique needs.

The college student or the young career person enjoys thought-provoking discussions on world affairs, marriage, philosophy, and theology. He needs friends who will accept him as he is. Sometimes he worries about finances, job opportunities, and his future mate. He wants to be of service and should be encouraged to teach in the Sunday school, participate in the choir or orchestra, and become involved in ushering, the bus ministry, camp counseling, VBS, visitation, etc.

The divorced person has suffered rejection, and may be dealing with child-custody and child-rearing problems. He needs someone who will listen nonjudgmentally. All too often the church has compounded the hurt rather than alleviating it. Instruction is needed in child rearing, finances, emotional readjustment, spiritual growth, and reconciliation with the former spouse if he has not remarried.

The widow or widower is overcome by the loss of his friend, lover, and counselor. The church is often helpful and attentive at the time of death, but the widowed person soon feels excluded from the fellowship of couples. Widowed people may be reluctant at first to join a singles group, not wanting to admit to being single again.

The separated person is in a unique position; he is single but not single. Some are separated while they work out marital problems; others are separated because of employment, military service, or imprisonment. The separated person has freedom, finances, and time, as do other singles, but he is not free to date or consider marriage, therefore he is often alone. The church needs to offer both counseling and instruction.

Young Adults

About three-fourths of young adults live in urban areas, constituting 14 percent of the typical United States city. More than age, *adjustment* is the criterion for defining a young adult.

Typically, young adults marry, permanently leave their parental home, complete their formal education, and become self-supporting. Now liberated from parental ties, they are often skeptical of previously accepted principles and values. They are searching for new principles or meaningful validation of old values. These adjustments bring new tasks for which most young adults have not been adequately trained, either formally or informally. During this period of life they typically learn to live with their mate, start a family, rear children, manage a budget and a home, get started in their occupation, take on civic responsibility, and find a congenial social group.[2]

The Sunday school can endear itself to young adults if it will train them for these new tasks. Husband/wife relationships, child rearing, discipline, and family budgeting can all be taught from practical and Biblical perspectives. The Sunday school should not only proclaim the Word of God, but also train young adults in methods of searching the Scriptures for themselves. Meaningful worship experiences lead to an honest encounter and fellowship with God, both corporately and privately. Ample opportunities must be given for socialization at this age when fellowship is urgently needed and can furnish spiritual encouragement.

Middle Adults

Most likely this age-group is the backbone of your church and community. Although middle adults usually comprise only about one-fourth of the church, they greatly influence the other three-fourths.

Physically, middle adults possess less energy. They may be acquiring the "middle-aged spread," graying hair, and skin that is more coarse and wrinkled. Biologically, male sexual powers and abilities are waning, while female sexuality is climbing to its peak. These physiological changes often bring psychological stress of varying proportions.

Changes also occur sociologically. Often middle adults' parents are experiencing failing health, and their own children need help through adolescence. As their children leave home, the "empty nest" brings loneliness, and there is also the adjustment of being a grandparent. Many women go back into the marketplace with their work skills, while their husbands' vocations reach the peak in both demands and compensation. Opportunities abound for civic duties. Even so, middle adults often have more leisure than in earlier years. They prefer quieter events such as dinner parties, study groups, adult-education classes, travel, and leisure outings, as opposed to strenuous sports.[3] Hobbies, collections, and small-group activities with a few friends take precedence over large-group activities.

The church needs to offer instruction and counsel, bringing the principles of the Word of God to these life changes. Genuine worship experiences, opportunities for evangelization, social services, and social and recreational activities all bring God, His Word, and His church into everyday, meaningful relevance.

Senior Adults

The senior years provide great potential to grow spiritually. The pressures of time and responsibility are lessened. Life experiences give deeper meaning to Biblical teachings.

The need for interaction with others continues throughout one's life. Senior adults need to be loved, accepted, appreciated, and respected both as individuals and as a group. The loss of a companion often occurs during this time, bringing painful adjustment. Many feel alone, unwanted, and unloved. On the other hand, time, which was in earlier years at a premium, is now available for fellowship meetings, daytime prayer groups and Bible studies, potluck lunches, hobbies, church bus trips, picnics, and special church projects. Discussions, films, and audio and video cassettes can provide meaningful information regarding health, money management, and wills.

Society has defined older persons as useless and nonproductive. Nothing could be further from the truth. Often senior adults can perform any task that a younger church member can, but as a rule they have more time to be involved. Since the leadership positions in the church, community, and vocation that they once held often have been handed to the next generation, they need to be involved in service projects to avoid feeling completely left out. Just a few tasks for seniors include being an assistant teacher, helping newcomers and new converts, counseling, visiting shut-ins, and maintaining church property.

While most senior adults maintain their own homes, occasional help is needed with maintenance and repair jobs. If someone provides transportation to church or on a shopping trip, he should make it a time for fellowship rather than an act of charity.

---

[1]F. Franklyn Wise, "Christian Education of Youth," in *Exploring Christian Education*, ed. A. Elwood Sanner and A. F. Harper (Kansas City, MO: Beacon Hill Press, 1978), p. 274.

[2]Clifford V. Anderson, "The Nature and Needs of Young Adults," in *Adult Education in the Church,* ed. Roy B. Zuck and Gene A. Getz (Chicago: Moody Press, 1970), pp. 37,38.

[3]H. Norman Wright, "The Nature and Needs of Middle Adults," in *Adult Education in the Church,* ed. Roy B. Zuck and Gene A. Getz (Chicago: Moody Press, 1970), p. 49.

5

Understanding the Pupil's Individual Needs

> And Jesus, when he came out, saw much people, and was moved with compassion toward them, because they were as sheep not having a shepherd: and he began to teach them many things (Mark 6:34).

Jesus went where the people were. Even though "he went into the synagogue on the sabbath day" (Luke 4:16), He didn't stop there. At the Sea of Galilee, He saw "Simon called Peter, and Andrew his brother, casting a net into the sea" (Matthew 4:18), and He said to them, "Follow me" (Matthew 4:19). In the city of Capernaum, "he saw a man, named Matthew, sitting at the receipt of custom: and he saith unto him, Follow me" (Matthew 9:9). And in the province of Galilee, Jesus found Philip of the city of Bethsaida "and saith unto him, Follow me" (John 1:43).

Jesus was a guest in the house of Zaccheus (Luke 19:5), and attended a great feast in the house of Matthew, who was also called Levi (Luke 5:29). He visited at length by night with a Pharisee named Nicodemus (John 3:1-15), and at noonday He brought living water to the Samaritan woman at Jacob's well (John 4:5-15).

In the parable of the great supper, He commanded us to "go out into the highways and hedges, and compel them to come in, that my house may be filled" (Luke 14:23). We cannot fulfill our ministry of teaching in the Sunday school classroom during 1 hour of contact with our students on Sunday morning. First, we must go out and bring them in. Then, we must visit where they are so we can understand their needs. It is one thing to know the general age-level characteristics of our students (which we discussed in the preceding chapter); it is quite another thing to know each individual student—his needs, desires, ambitions, etc.

A general understanding of the emotional, mental, physical, and social needs of the students is vital to effective teaching. Likewise, a knowledge of the students' individual needs helps the teacher avoid discouraging or embarrassing those in the class.

What Does the Teacher Need to Know?

Obtain personal data for each student. In addition to the usual information—name, address, and birth date—the teacher should keep a record of any contacts he makes. This record should show the date, type of contact, and any apparent results. The observation forms at the end of chapter 9 can be used to record information regarding the physical, emotional, social, and spiritual needs of each student.

Learn the secular educational level of each pupil. This information is essential in planning classroom activities and in making assignments according to the pupils' abilities.

Gain information on the employment of your pupils. What do their jobs require of them in hours, strength, education, training, etc.? This information will make the teacher more considerate of and helpful to his pupils. Many church activities require money. If a pupil is hard pressed financially, he may be embarrassed and may mask his problem behind a cloak of disinterest.

Learn the family relationships of your students. What are their responsibilities to their families? Understanding the family as a unit enables the teacher and the church to minister to them as well as to the individual pupil. It is not uncommon for an entire family to be won by the loving interest of a concerned Sunday school teacher.

Be aware of the students' activities and responsibilities both inside and outside the church. This knowledge not only provides a key to the pupils' interests, but may also give the teacher insight into the cause of an apparent lack of interest in church activities. Some students need extra prayer and require guidance regarding their choice of activities.

Determine each pupil's knowledge of the Bible and spiritual experience. Some pupils have superb Biblical knowledge, while others have barely read God's Word. Some have achieved steady spiritual growth, while others have not yet accepted Christ's salvation. This knowledge will be of immense benefit to the teacher in preparing lessons to edify the majority of his students. But only the leading of the Holy Spirit can guide those truths to meet individual needs.

How Does the Teacher Obtain This Data?

Through questioning and observation. Most students do not mind completing a simple form requesting needed information. Visits with students should be informal and conducted with considerable tact to avoid the appearance of prying. The interview should not be the focal point of the visit. Usually a student will welcome an informal time with his Sunday school teacher in his or the teacher's home, or over refreshments at a restaurant. For the teacher's ministry to be the most effective, he must not only *know* the individual, but also *care* about him. He must be familiar with the student's problems, have an understanding of his hopes and dreams, and be able to love him with sincere Christian love. A tone of Christian caring must be central during the visit.

Through parent-teacher visits. These visits can be conducted at the church on a scheduled basis or in connection with a Sunday school open house. However, the most valuable information is gained through a visit to the student's home. This allows the teacher to become better acquainted with the parents and lets them know of his interest and concern for the pupil. We must not assume that because the student has "always been in this church" or because "his father is a church deacon" that a home visit is unnecessary. How well do *you* know the student and his family? The teacher must be a good listener and learn how to better minister to the needs of the student and his family.

Through observation conducted in visits to the student's place of employment or school. Good judgment must be used in making such a visit. The home, job, and school are the real world that occupy 167 hours per week of the student's time. We have the remaining 1 hour per week in the Sunday school class to help him face his world with the confidence that only Christ can give!

Through observation during class social functions. Since fellowship is such a vital function of the Sunday school, the teacher should make frequent opportunities for such activities. An informal get-together in the teacher's home will give the students a better understanding of him and his environment. It also allows opportunity for more time together. A field trip, sporting event, picnic, or campout afford quality time to develop teacher-student relationships. Of course, fellowship functions can also be conducted at the church.

All of this information should be recorded and kept in a student folder that can be passed on from one teacher to the next as the student progresses in the Sunday school. Frequent reference to this data is of inestimable value in lesson preparation and in ministry to the students as individuals.

Self-esteem

It is impossible for a teacher to model and disciple Christianity in 1 hour of classroom time each week. Time must be spent with the students outside of the classroom. When a teacher is willing to spend time with a student during the week, two additional benefits are found: (1)the student's self-esteem is built, and (2)classroom discipline problems are often solved. Let us first consider the matter of self-esteem.

It is generally agreed that self-esteem is how a person feels about himself. It is the reflection of himself to himself. When a person has positive self-esteem, he owns one of life's most important possessions.

Self-esteem affects every area of life. It influences how a person relates to himself, God, and others. His thoughts, activities, and even his choice of friends are determined by the way he feels about himself. It also affects how he responds to the teacher and to others in the classroom.

Since a person's self-esteem begins forming in infancy and is constantly affected by his relationships with those around him, our students enter the classroom with varying self-images. Even though parents play the major role in helping children develop good feelings about themselves, the relationships we establish with our students can be a powerful force in helping them have a positive self-image.

Ingredients of Self-esteem

Self-esteem consists of four central ingredients: (1)worth, (2)confidence, (3)security, and (4)love. Having a sense of *worth* enables a person to believe that he is of significance and has personal value. David's knowledge that the Creator of the universe gave personal attention to intricately forming him in his mother's womb was a boost to his self-esteem (Psalm 139:13-18).

An individual who possesses *confidence* has a sense of inner strength and trusts his abilities. He is capable of reaching out, trying new tasks, and tackling new challenges. Realizing that God has given us all unique abilities and potential (1 Corinthians 12:4-7), the confident person rests in the knowledge that his gifts are valuable for building up the Body, even though they are different from those possessed by others.

Closely tied to a feeling of confidence is the need for a feeling of *security*. Whereas confidence is an internal feeling ("I can do it!"), security is based more on external conditions—the individual's environment and his relationship to it. A feeling of security enables a person to relax in the knowledge that his world is a safe place to be. Romans 8:38,39 refers to a solid foundation on which we can base our feeling of security.

Probably the feeling of being *loved* is the most important of the ingredients of self-esteem. If a person is to go through life happy and with the strength to cope with its problems and challenges, he must have the assurance that he is loved and accepted. The understanding that even before we were born God loved us (John 3:16), reinforces our feeling of being loved.

A person's self-esteem should be Bible-based, since God's Word never changes. Our relationships with those around us are constantly in flux, causing us to have mixed feelings about ourselves. But when we establish our self-esteem on what the unchangeable Word says, we can rest in the feelings of *worth, confidence, security,* and *love* God supplies!

Suggestions for Teachers

Now that we have considered the four main ingredients of self-esteem and realized that together with the parents we can cooperate to help our students have good feelings about themselves, let us focus our attention on some ways this can be accomplished.

Unfortunately, our society places undue importance on the "three Bs"—beauty, brains, and brawn. Those who are average or below average in these areas go almost unnoticed. It is the teacher's responsibility to help every student realize that he is significant because he was created in the image of God! The teacher should look for other attributes, such as a child's good humor, pleasant disposition, integrity, punctuality, considerateness, and willingness to persevere. Many qualities besides the "three Bs" are worth complimenting.

It is so easy to love the beautiful, intelligent, and strong. We must look beyond the runny nose, torn shirt, and tieless shoes to the child within and love him with God's love! The world looks very different to a child, and his perspective is just as valid as ours. We need to ask God to help us look at the world through the eyes of each student in our classroom. Of course, this can best be accomplished by spending quality time with each pupil in his own environment.

A person's confidence is aided when we express expectations based on his age-level characteristics, background, and pressures. For example, we must not demand that all students (even adults) read aloud in class. The student with a reading disability will feel threatened by this and may be discouraged from returning to class. Rather, we must help him compensate for his weakness by finding activities in which he can excel. If he is talented in art, for example, we can involve him in creating a poster, banner, or puppet relating to the lesson's topic. This activity substitution can be a powerful counterforce to feelings of inferiority.

Feelings of security are aided when the teacher communicates his belief in the student. We must be sure that our actions agree with our words. It is very confusing when the statement, "I believe you can do that, John," is accompanied by facial expressions of doubt.

Since the younger child believes *everything* an adult says, teasing can be very threatening to his sense of security. The adolescent doesn't always appreciate being teased either, especially if he is already unsure of himself because of his awkwardness and changing voice.

We must develop the habit of giving each student our undivided attention as frequently as possible. Eye contact assures him that he is the focus of your complete attention, helping him to be sure of your loving concern.

Praise—whether in the form of recognition or a compliment—for an achievement or some specific acceptable behavior, reinforces appropriate conduct. On the other hand, shaming a child for unacceptable behavior damages his sense of self-worth and should be avoided. We need to ask the Holy Spirit to sharpen our awareness and sensitivity.

Classroom Discipline

Since many discipline problems in the classroom are caused by those who suffer from low self-esteem, let us now turn our attention to discipline in the classroom.

What Is Discipline?

Webster's New Collegiate Dictionary gives many definitions for *discipline.* One of them states that it is "training that corrects, molds, or perfects." Another says *discipline* is a "system of rules governing conduct or action." We could say that *discipline* is the introduction of control into the life of a child or adult.

The purpose of discipline is to encourage the child to grow into adulthood with an adequate view of himself in relationship to God and others. When this is accomplished, the child attains a freedom to develop into the unique individual that God wants him to be. He is able to know who he is, why he is, and where he is going.

Of course, parents have the greatest responsibility for providing "training that corrects, molds, or perfects." But Sunday school teachers and workers play a very important role, too. The students who attend our classes exhibit varying degrees of disciplined behavior, which is indicative of the examples they have learned to emulate both at home and while they are under our weekly influence.

Environmental Influences

The conditions in the classroom affect student discipline. When the students step into a well-organized room and are greeted by a teacher who has the love of God emanating from him, they are motivated to exhibit the kind of behavior that is expected. Adequate facilities won't guarantee acceptable behavior, but crowded, stuffy, or cluttered rooms that are too hot or too cold tend to produce the opposite.

The Pupil

The *pupil* is the one for whom we are attempting to provide "training that corrects, molds, or perfects." It is our responsibility to learn the reasons why each pupil exhibits the behavior that he does.

What is his home environment? Students from difficult

home situations often misbehave to get the attention, recognition, and love that they are otherwise lacking.

What is his health status? The student who does not feel good or has a vision or hearing defect may be incapable of behaving as we expect.

Does he have a learning disability? The wise teacher will not expect all the students to perform in the same manner.

Does he have a sense of failure? A classroom presents a threatening situation to some students. The teacher must provide tasks that allow the student to experience success.

Older students should be given a voice in forming rules, but the fewer rules the better. Students have a sense of fairness and will respond very favorably to guidelines that they have helped formulate.

The Teacher's Responsibility

Even though the major responsibility for discipline lies with the parents, the way the teacher fulfills his teaching duties affects the discipline in the classroom. He who would positively affect his students for Christ must himself be disciplined. This involves commitment to adequate planning, lesson preparation, and personal spiritual growth. The teacher must employ a variety of teaching/learning techniques and provide interesting class activities. He must spend time with his students on an individual basis, visiting them in the familiar surroundings of their home to gain insight into behavior exhibited in the Sunday school class. The teacher should be in the classroom several minutes ahead of the required arrival time to have all preparations made before the advent of the "early birds."

Principles for Effective Discipline

There are three relatively simple principles that will aid effective discipline among our Sunday school students. The first of these is *clarity.* It is our responsibility as teachers to let our students know from the beginning what is expected of them while they are in the classroom. Children cannot be held accountable when they have not been told or do not understand what is acceptable behavior.

Next is the principle of *consistency*. Children need the security that comes with knowing the rules and knowing that they will be the same from one Sunday to the next. We must say what we mean and mean what we say. It is important that discipline not be determined by our mood, but by prearranged guidelines.

Finally, effective discipline is guided by a sense of *fairness*. Understanding the age-level characteristics of our students (which were discussed in the preceding chapter) will help us to form fair expectations.

Suggestions for Effective Discipline

Let us now consider a few practical suggestions that will help establish a good learning environment:

Nonverbal communication. (1)Eye contact—Simply making eye contact with the pupil who is exhibiting unacceptable behavior often corrects him. (2)Finger directives—Touching your finger to your lips lets the pupil know that you are requesting his silence. Pointing your finger to the workbook page reminds him that he should be working on the assigned exercise. (3)Silence—Your stopping while telling the story or giving instructions to the class will let the pupil know you are aware of his behavior. (4)Position movement—Without saying anything, simply move nearer the disruptive pupil. Laying a loving but firm hand on his arm or shoulder may be all that is required to redirect his attention.

Verbal messages. (1)Quietly call the pupil's name and follow it with one of the previously mentioned nonverbal directives. (2)In the flow of the story you are telling or the directions you are giving, quietly call the name of the pupil. It is important that your voice remain calm and deliberate. Sometimes a teacher allows his voice to rise in pitch and intensity when he is dealing with a problem. The opposite has a more calming effect.

Action. (1)Move the disruptive student to an area in the room where his inappropriate behavior will not be reinforced by other students. (2)Ask the student to wait (very briefly) outside the room until you or a helper can speak with him.

Preventive Measures

We feel it is better to approach classroom control from the positive side. The following suggestions can often avoid unpleasant disciplinary ordeals:

1. Begin the class on time and provide presession activities, such as those used in learning centers, for students who arrive early. (This will be discussed further in chapter 7.)

2. Provide periods of activity, alternated with quiet times. Think through these changes step by step.

3. Be thoroughly prepared, well-rested, and prayed up.

4. Provide instructions that are easily understood by the pupils. Misunderstanding leads to confusion, and confusion is the forerunner of total chaos.

5. Being well-groomed helps gain the respect of your pupils. They find it easier to obey someone for whom they have respect, and respect is earned, not demanded.

6. Ignore unintentional or insignificant behavior. Only deal with misbehavior that has become disruptive and interferes with another pupil's learning.

7. Be objective. Don't react out of bias or prejudice. Ask the Lord to help you demonstrate genuine love, concern, and interest for all your pupils, even those with stringy hair and an unpleasant odor.

8. Employ adequate help. Prospective teachers can serve an apprenticeship by being aides to master teachers.

9. Praise acceptable behavior. Children are so anxious to please their teachers that such comments as, "I like the way Jennifer is putting away the books," will work wonders. Praising acceptable behavior is one of the most effective and positive measures a teacher can use.

10. The wise teacher makes learning a joy. Discipline

problems diminish when pupils are provided with meaningful activities that relate to the lesson's objective.

11. The public school or Christian school teacher can be a valuable resource person to help you cope with a disruptive Sunday school pupil. That teacher has the child in his room many more hours during the week than you do on Sunday. He may be able to give you some helpful advice.

12. When all else fails, place the incorrigible pupil in the tutoring custody of another adult in some other room of the church. This adult should teach the lesson to this one child or visit with him in any way possible. Certainly, the pupil should not be isolated in a room by himself. After a few such sessions, the child may be able to successfully return to the normal classroom situation.

6

Learning and the Ministry of Teaching

Jesus stooped down, and with his finger wrote on the ground (John 8:6).

Learning is a process of growth; an adjustment to one's environment; a modification of experience, behavior, or conduct; and a change in attitude. Martha Leypoldt summarized it in the title of her book: *Learning Is Change.*[1] "The pupil has not learned until his head, heart, and life are changed by what he has learned."[2]

Beginning at birth, a baby perceives tiny bits of information through the physical senses—hearing, sight, touch, taste, and smell. A number of such impressions become fixed in the mind as a general concept. These concepts are referred to by the mind as fixed principles. The mind then acquires related information and organizes it in relationship to the primary learning. Finally, attitudes are developed about the facts that have been acquired.

The goal of the Sunday school is to produce mature Christians. This involves teaching, winning, nurturing, and training. Bible facts are foundational, but if we are to attain the goal of Christian maturity, students must advance beyond Biblical knowledge to doctrinal understanding, application of the truth, and change in their lives. (See Romans 12:2.)

Lawrence O. Richards identified five levels of learning in his book *Creative Bible Teaching*:[3]

1. *Rote learning*—the ability to repeat information from

memory without necessarily thinking about its meaning (such as repeating a memory verse, a prayer, or a catechism).

2. *Recognition*—the ability to understand the meaning of a concept (such as a beatitude).

3. *Restatement*—the ability to think through a concept and restate it in one's own words.

4. *Relation*—the ability to relate a concept to life (such as seeing how a beatitude would apply to a real-life situation).

5. *Realization*—the ability to apply a concept in one's daily life (such as actually changing one's behavior because of the concept).

Obviously, Christian education's goal is for the student to attain the level of *realization.* However, before that level can be reached, he must grow through the four preceding levels of learning.

Principles of Learning

Readiness

As we learned in chapter 4, chronological age to a large degree determines a student's readiness to learn. Physical, mental, emotional, and spiritual growth prepares the student to study subjects that earlier were neither understandable nor needed.

Students learn best when they are "in the mood" to learn. Therefore, it is the responsibility of the teacher to provide an atmosphere that is conducive to learning by asking questions, posing problems, or using discussion to help the students realize their needs. The teacher must move from the students' *felt* or realized needs to their *real* or unrealized needs. Obviously, the teacher must move from the known to the unknown; helping the students see the relationships of the parts to the whole.

Motivation

Learning must not only be meaningful to a student's needs,

but also bring him personal satisfaction. "If the pupil derives pleasure from learning, he will want to continue to learn."[4] He must succeed and enjoy Sunday school experiences *soon* after he begins attending or enters a new class. Public school teachers, for example, are extremely saddened to see a first grader fail to enter second grade with the rest of his class. If it is necessary to hold back a student, it is better to do it in the second grade. The old saying, "Nothing succeeds like success," is true.

Since all students are not the same, they should not be expected to do the same work. The teacher should assign work so that it is *possible* for a student to succeed. This is true not only of the Bible study itself, but also of other Sunday school expectations (such as offerings, regular attendance, etc.).

There are two kinds of motivation: intrinsic and extrinsic. Intrinsic motivation is that which comes from inside. Our goal is to instill ideals and value within students that will motivate them to do what should be done because "real needs" have become "felt needs." On the other hand, extrinsic motivation is that which comes from outside. Praise, blame, prizes, honor rolls, etc., are forms of extrinsic motivation. Other forms of extrinsic motivation, though less obvious, are the desire for social approval, the wish to be "first," the longing to possess, the desire to be like others, etc.

We have long understood that children need extrinsic motivation, and we have provided it to some degree. However, we often cringe at the idea of such materialistic motivation for adults. Yes, we should be intrinsically motivated; we should work for Jesus' kingdom because it is a "real need." But both children and adults are still human beings. Not all have reached the "realization" level of learning. We must remember what Paul said: "I am made all things to all men, that I might by all means save some" (1 Corinthians 9:22).

Memory

Learning is based on the principle that at least part of our experiences is retained in the conscious memory. We noted earlier that we learn through our senses—hearing, sight, touch, taste, and smell. The more senses that are activated, the stronger the impression, and the more likely that impression will be retained in our conscious memory.

Memory is also strongly aided by muscular activity. No amount of listening to a lecture on how to play the piano, listening to records of piano music, seeing slides or movies of the piano being played, or feeling the piano keyboard will ever produce a pianist. The muscles must be activated to feed information back to the brain for storage. The same is true of other so-called "mental-only learning." It is for this reason that teachers sometimes ask their students to write something several times. These laws of learning do not change, regardless of age. A 50-year-old learns basically the same way a 50-day-old learns.

The following are some commonly accepted figures regarding a pupil's ability to retain information when various "sensorial" impressions are made and when student activity is involved:[5]

The Pupil's Ability to Retain Information

10% of what he *hears* or *reads*—called *verbalization*—using words, symbols, and other abstractions (like hearing a speaker or reading a book).

30% of what he *sees*—called *visualization*—using pictures of real life (like seeing slides).

50% of what he *sees and hears*—called *audiovisualization*—using representations of real life (like watching a movie).

70% of what he *sees, hears, and says*—called *dramatization*—using made-up experiences (like roleplaying or making a model).

90% of what he *sees, hears, says, and does*—called *actualization*—using real-life experiences (like doing a project, taking a trip, or witnessing to a friend).

Method of Teaching	*Recall After 3 Hours*	*Recall After 3 Days*
Telling alone	70%	10%
Showing alone	72%	20%
Telling & showing	85%	65%

Notice that *seeing* is a stronger sensorial impression than *hearing.* When these two are combined, the effect is even greater. Of course, if the sensorial impressions of taste, smell, and touch are also used, the impression becomes even more vivid. Now observe in the preceding figures how much *saying* and *doing* aid the learning process. The more muscles involved in the activity, and the longer the time of activity, the stronger will be the muscular impression and the greater will be the memory retention.

An adapted Chinese proverb says: "I hear, and I forget. I see, and I remember. I do, and I understand."

Other factors in memory are association, meaningfulness, and repetition. Students learn more if the new material is linked to previously learned information. The new material must be understandable, and reviews should be frequent but brief.

Teaching

According to D. V. Hurst, teaching "is first arousing the pupil to want to learn and then guiding him in that learning process. . . . It requires that both the teacher and pupil engage in mental activity. The two must cooperate in a common experience centered in common interest."[6]

What Teaching Is Not

We can learn much about what teaching is by first seeing what it is not:

Teaching is not telling. Perhaps the most overused teaching method is the lecture. Of course, it is impossible to think of learning without the impartation of the teacher's knowledge to his students; however, just as listening is not necessarily learning, telling is not necessarily teaching.

Teaching is not an aimless, open discussion. This misconception of teaching aims at nothing and hits it! Teaching must be both sensitive to the students' needs and encouraging of their active participation in the learning process, but the learning process must be guided by the teacher.

Teaching is not using everything in the quarterly. Almost any curriculum is written with lesson materials to cover any situation from a Sunday school of five pupils to one of 5,000. Obviously, much of any lesson's material will not apply in a particular situation. A wise teacher chooses only two or three learning activities and covers them so thoroughly that the lesson's central theme is truly learned.

Teaching is not the impartation of knowledge and the drilling of those facts into the mind. Facts are very important, but if teaching is to change lives, the knowledge must be related to everyday problems; showing how Biblical principles apply.

Teaching is not activity for activity's sake. The concept being taught determines the method; the method should not determine the concept. Of course, we appreciate teachers who use innovative teaching methods, but there must be balance.

Teaching is not coming to the class with no advance planning or preparation and trusting the Lord for something to say. This approach may seem very spiritual, but according to God's Word, it is not correct (2 Timothy 2:15). If God can guide while we are teaching, can He not also anoint while we are preparing?

What Teaching Is

Since none of the preceding concepts is satisfactory, what is teaching? Earlier in this chapter we learned that the student learns best when he is ready and motivated. He remembers best when a maximum number of the five senses have been stimulated and when student activity has been employed. A student learns the *least* when he is reading or hearing symbols, and the *most* when he is actually participating.

It would appear, therefore, that the teacher should be one who cares for his students, is a motivator, and is a coordinator, guiding the learning process. This kind of teaching helps the students experience truth.

Teaching is caring. Teachers must become concerned about and involved with their students on a personal level in order to understand their needs. As teachers, we must exhibit truth in our lives. Students learn more about God by what their teachers *are* and *do* than by what they *say.* Findley B. Edge has said: "The single most important factor that influences learning is the life and personality of the teacher."[7]

Teaching is motivating. Students must be motivated to attend Sunday school, prepare their assignments, and participate in class activities. This can best be accomplished with lessons for which the pupils are ready—lessons that concern them and their needs. Teachers should not fear using extrinsic motivation (praise, prizes, awards, etc.). As spiritual concepts are learned, the students will value the things of God so highly that intrinsic motivation will be activated.

Teaching is coordination. Once the students are cared for and motivated to learn, their efforts must be coordinated. Goals must be set; encouraging them to seek truth. The teacher must then make assignments that will help the students discover answers. He must plan other student activities, share the information he knows, and show how these principles apply to life. The students do the learning, but the teacher must create an environment conducive to learning.

All this is called "guided learning." Students are helped to experience truth as they actively participate and the teacher is active as a guide.

Teaching Tools

"A workman is not better than his tools"—so goes the old

saying. To some degree this is true of Sunday school teachers. The tools of our trade are the curriculum, the classroom, and audiovisual aids.

The Curriculum

Sunday school curriculum provides a systematic study of the Bible and church doctrine. As a graded study, it takes into account the needs, interests, and capabilities of the various age-levels. Curriculum is based on the "building block" theory, which means that each age-level of study builds on the previous material. For this reason, it is not good to use several different publishers' curriculums in one church's school. Such mixing results in both overlapping and omission of essential spiritual concepts.

Radiant Life curriculum, published by Gospel Publishing House, serves the above purposes and more. There are at least four reasons why we recommend this material:

1. It is Biblically accurate and doctrinally complete for Pentecostal churches. If we desire that our students learn the full gospel, it is essential that we provide a Sunday school curriculum that teaches it.

2. The teaching aids are creative, yet flexible. Many teaching ideas are presented, allowing a choice of methods to meet each situation.

3. It is competitively priced. Private studies have shown that comparable Radiant Life materials are almost always less expensive than other publishers' curriculums.

4. It is produced by the Assemblies of God publishing house. All profits go into the ministries of our Fellowship. Profits from other publishers may go to their owners and stockholders, but certainly not to our ministries.

> But to be effective, curriculum must be properly used. Two common errors in using curriculum are to follow it too closely or not closely enough. . . . It should be used as a tool to aid the teacher in his study and development of the lesson.[8]

The Classroom

"Next to the personality of the teacher, the classroom environment is the most important influence on the pupil."[9] The church building and grounds need not be the largest or most ostentatious in town, but their grooming and maintenance speak volumes in a single glance. Classroom improvement should be a part of the annual Sunday school budget, because the classroom teaches even when we do not. In some situations the surroundings speak so loudly that the pupils cannot hear what the teacher says.

Today's economics dictate that church facilities be used often and in many ways. For example, one area may serve for recreation and dining and also house the junior department. Another area could house the youth department, serve as the prayer chapel, and provide a place to conduct the youth service during the week. Departmental activity areas could be used for Royal Rangers and Missionettes meetings. Many churches today also use classroom space during the week for day care and Christian school ministries. All this emphasizes that a Sunday school classroom is not the private domain of any one teacher, but must be shared by the total ministries of the church.

Multiple ministries necessitate efficient use of space. Adequate shelving and storage cabinets help organize supplies, preserve floorspace by using cubit feet rather than square feet, and give a neat appearance.

Audiovisual equipment dictates that lighting be controllable. Room-darkening window coverings are a must, as are dimable lights. Light fixtures, therefore, need to be incandescent rather than fluorescent, and the switches should control only small areas.

Folding partitions and movable room dividers serve to maximize the use of an area. Many churches are now removing permanent partitions that once limited classroom usage.

Listed on the next page is the recommended square feet per pupil in a classroom:

30-35—Cradle roll and nursery
25-30—Beginner
20-25—Elementary
12-15—Junior and senior high
10-12—Young adult and adult

Classroom furniture and equipment should have quality and be designed to permit flexible usage. For example, trapezoid-shaped tables can be used individually; by putting several together in a straight line, two together in a hexagon or an hourglass shape, or four together in the shape of a horseshoe; or by combining four of them to make a single big table. Adjustable legs make these tables usable in several different age-level classes.

Here are the recommended heights (in inches) of chairs and tables for each age-level:

Chairs	*Tables*	*Age-level*
6-8	16-18	Cradle roll
8-10	18-20	Nursery
10-12	20-22	Beginner
12-14	22-24	Primary
13-15	23-25	Middler
15-17	25-27	Junior
18	28	Junior high
		Adult

It is so easy to accumulate little unsightly piles of "stuff" here and there. A good cleaning and reorganization makes for immediate improvement, but beyond that, both short- and long-range goals should be set for classroom improvement. Every teacher should answer these three questions:

1. What obvious changes can I make in my Sunday school area?
2. What changes can be made at little or no expense?
3. Which changes can I make immediately?

Audiovisual Tools

Audio tools include records and record players, and cassette and reel-to-reel tape recorders and players. *Visual aids* are classified as "nonprojected" and "projected." *Nonprojected visual aids* include the chalkboard, flannel board, felt board, objects, charts, graphs, maps, globes, various kinds of paintings and drawings, puppets, and newspapers and magazines. The list, of course, could go on. *Projected visual aids* include slides, filmstrips, overhead projections, and silent movies. *Audiovisual aids* include a combination of sound and sight, such as slides and a cassette tape or record, filmstrips and a cassette tape or record, and sound movies.

Please note that in audiovisual lingo, "hardware" refers to equipment, such as a record player, tape player, projector, screen, etc. "Software" refers to materials such as records, tapes, slides, movies, etc.

Earlier in this chapter we learned that students remember concepts more easily if they are presented vividly, with a number of "sensorial" impressions being made. For example, five times as much is remembered with an audiovisualization as with a verbalization.

We would think it strange today to see a carpenter use only a handsaw to cut every board while constructing a house. It would be even stranger for him to use only an ax to cut the boards. Both the ax and the handsaw are useful, and at one time these were the only tools he had available. But without the electric saw, today's carpenter would be much less efficient.

The Media Center

With these facts before us, why do so many Sunday school teachers still make inadequate use of these teaching tools? We have found four common reasons: (1)"I don't know where to get it." (2)"I don't know how to operate the equipment." (3)"It's too expensive." (4)"It's too much effort."

A Sunday school "media center" helps solve most of these problems. A media center is a collection of study materials, teaching aids, and equipment designed to help the Sunday school teacher. It usually includes library items such as books, reference materials, and magazines, along with audiovisual equipment and supplies, picture files, maps, puppets, handcraft supplies, etc. These materials are usually set up in a separate room or storage area. A few pieces of plywood can be used to construct a media center storage cabinet.

One person can operate the media center for all but the larger Sunday schools. This worker should first collect existing equipment from all over the church, survey its condition, catalog it, and store it. Then he can recommend what additional equipment is needed. In a staff meeting, he should give instruction on how to operate each piece of equipment. Some individual instruction also may be needed. Finally, he should keep all hardware and software in good repair.

With the teachers, he should survey the upcoming quarter's curriculum and purchase or rent appropriate software. Then both hardware and software may be sent to the classrooms on a sign-out basis. A card catalog is an excellent control tool.

Now let us return to the reasons given for not using audiovisual teaching tools to see how the media center will solve these problems.

1. "*I don't know where to get it.*" The media center takes this responsibility from the teacher and gives it to the church's specialist in this field.

2. "*I don't know how to operate the equipment.*" The media center coordinator gives instruction and then watches as each teacher practices. Earlier in this chapter we learned that students learn best by doing. So do teachers! There is simply no better way to learn to operate audiovisual hardware than by doing it!

3. "*It's too expensive.*" The media center reduces costs by making maximum usage of the equipment a church does have. But in the final analysis, is it a matter of finances or priorities? For example, the amount of money that some churches spend on a sound system could buy 50 overhead projectors.

4. "*It's too much effort.*" Yes, it takes effort, but if we feel

strongly enough about our ministry of teaching to prepare a lesson at all, why not prepare it in such a manner that it will be remembered and make a change in the lives of our students? (So that a teacher will not be embarrassed during his class period, he should preview and study any program he will use.)

---

[1]Martha Leypoldt, *Learning Is Change* (Valley Forge, PA: Judson Press, 1971).

[2]Ronald G. Held, *Learning Together* (Springfield, MO: Gospel Publishing House, 1976), p. 32.

[3]Adapted from Lawrence O. Richards, *Creative Bible Teaching* (Chicago: Moody Press, 1968), pp. 69-73.

[4]D. V. Hurst, *And He Gave Teachers* (Springfield, MO: Gospel Publishing House, 1955), p. 101.

[5]Held, *Learning Together,* pp. 34-36.

[6]Hurst, *And He Gave Teachers,* p. 97.

[7]Findley B. Edge, *Teaching for Results* (Nashville, TN: Broadman Press, 1956), p. 223.

[8]Held, *Learning Together,* p. 87.

[9]*Ibid.*

7

Early Childhood and Elementary Teaching Methods

Suffer little children to come unto me, and forbid them not: for of such is the kingdom of God (Luke 18:16).

As Sunday school teachers in the early childhood and elementary departments, we want to reach our students with the message that God loves and cares for them and we do too. The means we choose to communicate this message are the *method.* Numerous methods are available, but it is important that we be familiar and comfortable with those we choose.

Storytelling

Storytelling is probably the oldest and most used method with children of all ages. A danger is overuse; forgetting to use other excellent methods.

Storytelling requires an awareness of the age-level characteristics of the audience (which were discussed in chapter 4). The vocabulary in the story should be easily understood by the listeners. Very young children enjoy short stories that include many *action* words (such as run, jump, play, eat, sing, and sleep), and *name* words (such as baby, sister, mother, dog, John, and kitten).

Repetition of words and ideas is very important with young children. They feel comfortable and secure with the familiar, such as hearing the same story again and again.

Through his imagination, the young child becomes a part of the story. Always distinguish between *real* and *make-believe* stories. Older children identify with the hero of a story, so be sure the stories used have heroes worthy of their emulation.

Preparation

The secret of good storytelling is simple: Learn the story so well that it becomes part of you. Read it several times, but do not attempt to memorize it. Be able to put the story into your own words, using expressions with which you are comfortable and that will be understood by your audience. Plan the opening and closing sentences—these are the only part of the story that you should memorize.

A variety of visual aids will enhance your story. You may use the flash cards that came with the story, or you may choose a few appropriate slides. If you have artistic ability, draw a simple sketch on the chalkboard. Check the picture file that you have gathered from old Sunday school curriculum, greeting cards, magazines, and posters to provide resources. You could also use an overhead transparency picture. An object related to the story can generate excitement. Remember that children want to touch, so the object should be one that can be handled by them.

Keep the visual aids simple. Be sure that they remain just that—aids. Complicated visuals distract the audience and draw attention away from rather than to the story.

Telling a Story

Be sure that both you and your audience are comfortable before beginning your story. Sitting on a rug with the children around you puts everyone on the same level. A finger play or activity song prepares the children to listen.

Make it easy for your audience to listen to the story by using a conversational tone, and make it believable by having a sincere attitude. Vary the tempo and pitch of your voice occasionally. Voice tone can express the meanings of words. An air of expectancy can be created by a pause or facial expression.

Games

Younger elementary children find new interest in memorizing the Bible verse for the day if a game is employed. For example, the teacher can write the verse on the chalkboard or overhead transparency. After the children have read the verse, one of them can erase a word. Then a child can volunteer to read the verse, filling in the missing word. This continues until all of the words have been erased.

An example of a number game is to write on cards the numbers 66, 40, and 12. Ask the children of what they are reminded by each of these numbers. Sixty-six is the number of the Books in the Bible. Forty is the number of days it rained. Twelve is the number of Jesus' disciples.

Older elementary children enjoy puzzles, riddles, and other activities that require skill. This is an excellent time to use the Junior Bible Quiz Fact Pak. Popular table games and TV games can be adapted by using Bible characters and facts.

Games can be a highly successful method as children experience the fun of learning. They should not be used merely to entertain, but rather to communicate facts, change attitudes, and develop skills. "Games often set a mood for learning by relieving tensions and helping the children to work together as a group."[1]

Finger Plays

Finger plays calm the restless, prepare them for a story, prayer, worship time, or a rest period. Other finger exercises reinforce the Bible lesson's ideas in the tender minds of young children.

Often the nursery and beginner teacher quarterlies describe finger plays. Clip these and organize a file (just as you would save pictures). *Bible-Teaching Finger Plays,* by Marian White (Grand Rapids: Baker Book House), is an excellent source of finger plays.

As you study and use these exercises, they will become fixed in your memory. Then you can use them spontaneously to meet the demands of various classroom situations.

Creative Art Activities

Creative art activities can be used effectively as a teaching technique with children of almost any age. With adaptations and consideration for individual differences, such activities provide opportunities for children to express their God-given desire to make and do things.

Freehand drawing, clay modeling, freehand cutting, and paper tearing are examples of creative art activities. Remember to provide big pieces of paper and large crayons and pencils because the small muscles required for detail work have not yet developed in young children. This child's work may look like mere scribbling to you, but he should be allowed to try. Many attempts will bring improvement, and later he will be able to participate in more sophisticated activities and projects.

Creative art can be expanded with older children to include banners, posters, and murals. They enjoy making their activities cooperative ventures. These activities help the development of the whole child, aiding his sense of self-worth and making his Sunday school and church experiences enjoyable and pleasurable. They provide an opportunity for achievement in the church environment which lays a foundation for future years of service.

> Creative teaching helps to build self-confidence and courage in the shy, withdrawn child. It provides a worthy outlet for the restless, boisterous child. It creates a wholesome atmosphere for friendly working together as a group.[2]

Creative Writing

Children often have moments of creative inspiration when they can spontaneously compose a poem, story, or song. Their words should be captured and the children encouraged to draw illustrative pictures. While older children can write down their own ideas, the teacher must be the scribe for the younger ones; otherwise, their creative spark may be smothered with worry about the mechanics of writing and spelling.

Learn to listen to what the child says and how he says it, then write down the words exactly as they are spoken. A cassette tape recorder with a built-in microphone can pick up voices from an entire room.

Perhaps you are already recording your entire Sunday school class session. (This allows you to critique your teaching each week.) If you do make such a recording, a child's verbal composition will be on the tape. To transcribe it for the student, simply rewind the tape to the beginning of that section and write down every word the child said. Of course, the transcription should be done immediately.

Become sensitive to these creative periods and provide the materials and encouragement for further efforts. Since creative writing is an outgrowth of experiences the children have encountered, it is your responsibility to provide numerous experiences that will furnish such a background. Pictures, objects, films, or a brief walk outdoors may spark a child's creativity.

You may discover that one creative child will inspire the entire group to write a poem or prayer for worship time. Encourage your pupils to write letters to children of missionaries, notes to shut-ins or absentees, or thank-you letters to church workers who have visited or helped them. They may enjoy creating open-ended stories for roleplaying.

Older children find *Scripture paraphrasing* a meaningful experience. Putting verses into their own words can be accomplished without doing damage to the sacredness of the Bible. It challenges them to consider what the passage really means to them, as the third level of learning (restatement) is reached (as we discussed in the previous chapter).

Choral reading provides involvement by the entire group. Older children enjoy choosing a passage of Scripture on which they can base a script. Any Scripture portion may be used; however, the psalms lend themselves well to this exercise. When the script is written, the children should practice reading it smoothly and with expression. Group involvement promotes high interest and an excellent learning atmosphere.

The children can be challenged to "give it their best" if they have the opportunity to read for the adults.

The *newsstory* can be assigned as an out-of-class research project for older children or it can become an in-class individual or cooperative project. A Bible story is written as it might appear in today's local newspaper in the news, sports, advertisement, or society section.

The *parable* is the technique the Master Teacher utilized so often in His earthly ministry. Jesus used these simple, brief stories to help His audience bridge the gap between real-life situations and the concepts of His kingdom. The students can work on these alone or in small groups, using real-life situations of today to explain a scriptural principle.

Creative Drama

Creative drama can become a significant part of the teaching/learning experiences of your students. "Creative drama, sometimes referred to as educational drama or playmaking, is commonly used as a general term for any kind of play that utilizes the imagination, the great world of 'let's pretend.' "[3] Plays, pantomimes, shadow pictures, pageants, tableaus, puppets, and roleplaying are examples of creative drama. With adaptations these can be used with children of any elementary age.

Sunday morning is too brief to indulge in activity for activity's sake. The many-faceted values of creative drama make its place in the schedule justifiable, since children derive educational, recreational, devotional, cultural, and therapeutic benefits from this activity. The child becomes uninhibited as he acts out his inner feelings. Dramatization also sharpens the child's awareness and sensitivity to the needs of others, altering both his attitudes and behavior in this regard.

As with creative writing, the teacher is a guide or facilitator in the learning process, assuming a passive role. The attention is focused on the students, who are discovering truths from their own creativity while the teacher assists.

Music

Music is important to children of all ages. Through this universal language, the teacher and students develop a bond of common discovery, enjoyment, and worship.

Music is an effective means of communication with young children. Songs can be used to direct their activities. Their response to your *singing,* "Let's put away the books," will probably be prompter than to your *saying* the same thing. Quiet music reduces restlessness and brings relaxation.

When you are deciding which music to use, remember the age-level characteristics of the children (as we discussed in chapter 4). For example, songs for young children must be short and use vocabulary that can be easily understood. Because their voice range is limited and their vocal muscles are not well developed, the children should be encouraged to sing softly, since strained voices could result in possible permanent damage. The words should have strong appeal to the senses.

Music creates an atmosphere in which children find it easy to worship. It aids the expression of their feelings and attitudes about God, Jesus, and their faith. Carefully chosen songs can encourage the children to make a decision for Christ.

A piano is certainly not necessary to provide good musical experiences for your children. Even if you have no formal training and music is not your forte, don't panic. A cassette tape or a record can be effective. If you can use a piano, the melody should be played very simply, especially for younger children. It should be kept in tune, so they can form correct tone concepts.

Practicing with rhythm sticks, triangles, rattles, or drums helps children learn different sounds and create their own music and rhythm. These instruments can be constructed quite easily and economically.

Learning Centers

A learning center is a place where the child becomes involved in an activity that reinforces the lesson theme. Whether you refer to it as an interest center, activity center, learning station, or learning center, its purpose is the same: to provide opportunities for learning through a variety of experiences.

The learning center approach recognizes that each child has different abilities and needs. It is based on the knowledge that learning takes place through sensorial activity, as we discussed in the preceding chapter. The activity, curiosity, and short attention span of the young child require the informal, flexible program of learning centers.

There are a number of reasons why this approach is very effective. Well-planned and well-arranged learning centers challenge the child to explore, find an interest, and learn. Since the number of children present at one time should not exceed five to eight, more individual attention can be given. A teacher/helper's role changes from that of a transmitter of information to that of a guide or facilitator.

Class begins when the first child arrives on Sunday morning. He immediately goes to the learning center of his choice; those who arrive later join him or choose another center. No time is lost and discipline problems diminish because the child has a variety of exciting activities awaiting his arrival each week; promoting a positive attitude toward Sunday school.

Several learning centers can be created in a large open area, small classrooms can be converted into learning centers, with the children moving from room to room. The number of helpers and children in your department or class, as well as the available space, will determine the number of centers.

The learning centers can change from one Sunday to the next, depending on the purpose of the lesson. However, since young children are more secure with the familiar, learning centers for them should not be changed too often.

Well-written instructions for the activities at each center are a must. The vocabulary used should be easily read and understood. The teacher/helper will need to read the instructions to prereaders, or an audiocassette can be used to play prerecorded instructions.

The *housekeeping* center is a favorite among preschoolers. Here children learn to share and show kindness to others. They enjoy experimenting with adult roles, whereby they can act out many of the experiences they have encountered at home. Ladies' and men's clothing should be provided for dressing up. The furniture should be child-sized but not doll-sized. Wooden kitchen appliances, unbreakable food containers and dishes, a small table and chairs, a child-sized bed, and a rocking chair are useful.

In the *nature* center, all of the child's senses can be stimulated. He may *see* the fish in the aquarium, *hear* the roaring ocean in the shell, *smell* the fragrant rose, *taste* the delicious apple, or *touch* the prickly cactus. Items for the nature center are all around us. Birds, worms, turtles, frogs, toads, gerbils, and hamsters, are just a few of the living creatures you can provide, and many different plant varieties are available. Children benefit from experiences with nonliving items too, such as rocks, magnets, and fossils.

All children enjoy and benefit from the *puzzle* center. Small children appreciate the freedom of working on a puzzle while lying on the floor. If the floor is not carpeted, provide a small rug or carpet piece for each child. The age of the children determines the difficulty of the puzzles. Provide puzzles with varying degrees of difficulty, since you want every child to be both successful and challenged in his experiences at this center.

Older children may appreciate making their own puzzles. A research project for such a group could be to make a map of Paul's missionary journeys. Then they could cut it into pieces, jumble them, and see how long it takes to reconstruct their map.

The quiet, shy child may frequent the *book* center, which offers him rest and a feeling of security. Promote continued interest by rotating the books on display so that each Sunday a few new ones appear, but don't remove the favorites.

A *research* center contains a Bible, an atlas, a concordance, a Bible dictionary, and other resource materials for locating additional information related to the day's lesson. Be sure these are available to junior classes.

A *listening* center allows the children to hear music, stories, and poems that are lesson-related. Records or tapes can be used. The Canon Bible filmstrip library is correlated to the Radiant Life curriculum. Their "instant replay" feature provides story-review and life-application questions and discussion.

No doubt you have thought of other centers for your teaching/learning situation. Art, exercise, block, story, music, drama, viewing, and writing centers are all possibilities. Learning centers can best be used in the extended session scheduling; however, they can also be used quite effectively in the 1-hour session.

Younger children enjoy the freedom of moving from one center to another, so learning centers may be used throughout the entire schedule. It is better to have a predetermined schedule for older children, so you may use learning centers for only a part of the schedule. The class might meet together for the story, music, and worship, and then utilize the learning centers for listening and exercise.

If you are considering learning centers, it is advisable to begin by studying books and magazines containing more information about them. Arrange to visit a school or another church facility and observe a class where learning centers are used extensively. Discuss your questions with another teacher who has had experience with this approach.

It is best to start in one department, rather than attempting to change all the children's departments at the same time. Teachers, pupils, and parents, too, will appreciate ample time to adapt to the changes. It is also good to begin with just one or two learning centers.

Summary

We have certainly not exhausted the possible techniques that can provide teaching/learning experiences for early childhood and the elementary age-group. The list goes on—handwork, tests, assignments and reports, questions and answers, discussions, etc.

For further study we recommend chapter 10, "What Am I Going to Do Sunday?" in *A Handbook for Guiding the Elementary Child*, written by Ronald W. Clark. Early childhood teachers should study chapter 8, "How Do I Create the Learning Environment?" in *A Handbook for Guiding the Preschool Child*, by Sandy Askew. Both handbooks are published by Gospel Publishing House, Springfield, Missouri.

Some of the methods we have explored in this chapter may be among your favorites; others may be completely unfamiliar to you. We challenge you to try some new techniques. Choose one and study it. Perhaps you can observe another teacher using it effectively in his/her classroom, then put it to use yourself. You must try it before you can determine whether it will work for you.

After using a new teaching method, it is good to ask yourself two questions: (1)Did the children *learn*? (2)Did the children *enjoy* learning? If you can answer these two questions positively, make repeated use of that technique.

Of course, you cannot expect to feel as comfortable with a new teaching/learning method as you do with one you have used since the first Sunday you taught. Teachers are just like children; the more familiar the situation, the more secure we are!

You will discover that your children will exhibit new enthusiasm and interest in Sunday school when they are offered a variety of activities in which they can become involved.

---

[1]Elizabeth B. Jones, *Teaching Primaries Today* (Grand Rapids: Baker Book House, 1974), p. 121.

[2]*Ibid.*, p. 91.

[3]D. V. Hurst, Dwayne E. Turner, and Samuel H. Henning, *Mastering the Methods* (Springfield, MO: Gospel Publishing House, 1979), pp. 84,85.

8

Youth and Adult Teaching Methods

> And they said one to another, Did not our heart burn within us, while he talked with us by the way, and while he opened to us the Scriptures? (Luke 24:32).

Just as learning should be a joy for children, so it should be for youth and adults. These students may attend Sunday school for a while because of coercion, duty, obligation, or expectation, but in the final analysis, they will attend because they want to and are fulfilled in the experience. Unless needs are met, youth and adults will not attend Sunday school.

Fellowship Aspects of Sunday School

Sunday school offers small-group fellowship, permits the personal touch, and provides a workable system of follow-up. It enhances the sense of belonging, as it allows for lay involvement in ministry and provides a training ground for future church leaders.

All other things being equal, people attend the church where they feel they belong and are an accepted, functioning part of the body. Efforts should be made to create an atmosphere of nonjudgmental love and mutual support. More than superficial "get-acquainted introductions" are required. The teacher of youth or adults must specifically plan for such social needs to be met. If facilities and cultural standards permit, before-class refreshments are a good icebreaker.

When the pupils are seated in rows of chairs or pews there is little opportunity for interaction. Sitting around tables is best, but sitting in chairs in a semicircle is the second choice. Opportunity for additional social support must be offered outside of Sunday school class time.

How Youth and Adults Learn

We learned in chapter 6 that retained learning results from strong, vivid sensorial impressions combined with activity. It is a profound mistake to think that because a person can read well and think for himself, he no longer responds to the same motivations or to personal involvement in the teaching/learning process. Actually, a youth or adult with more resources at his disposal can and should be more actively involved in this process than are children.

In almost any Sunday school lesson, several different teaching methods should be employed. When students can predict how a lesson will be taught, the teacher has become stale and needs to employ new methods. However, activity must not be used for activity's sake alone. There must be a definite learning objective for every segment of the lesson. As a general rule, 20 minutes is the maximum attention span for an adult. If for no other reason than this, two or three different methods should be used in each lesson.

Youth and Adult Electives

We are living in the age of continuing education. Schooling today is never completed. By the time some material is learned, it is outdated. Adults by the millions are enrolling in colleges, junior colleges, and high schools, for daytime or night classes on subjects from advanced computer programming to the art of Chinese cooking.

Two elements of college classes are often missing from Sunday school youth and adult classes. First, continuing education students enroll in classes in which they are interested. Until recently, our prescribed quarterly dictated the subject that would be studied regardless of students' needs or interests. Youth and adult electives have partially solved this problem. When deciding which Sunday school courses to teach, poll not only those persons who are presently attending your Sunday school, but also those who are not. Would they attend if interesting subjects were being taught?

The second missing element in many Sunday school classes is a sense of accomplishment. When a college course is completed, a grade is given the student by the teacher and is recorded on his transcript. Often Sunday school classes go on year after year with no recognition of a job well done.

There is one inherent danger in youth and adult elective classes. At the beginning of this chapter we learned that a primary benefit of the Sunday school is the small-group fellowship it provides. Adult classes bond into tight fellowship groups. When elective classes are introduced, those bonds are broken, as students gravitate toward various learning interests. The gradual introduction of electives will lessen this trauma, allowing time for new fellowship groups to form in the Sunday school structure.

Following are several effective teaching methods for youth and adults.

Assignment and Report

We have examined two common maladies of youth and adult classes. First, sometimes students are expected to study materials that neither interest them nor meet their needs. Second, sometimes they are deprived of the feeling of accomplishment by never "passing." A third common problem is a lack of student lesson preparation. This problem arises either because the teacher has not assigned study materials, or because the students are not held accountable to report on their lesson preparation.

Class members need to do more than listen; they must actively participate. The best learning comes by doing. When assignment reports are used near the beginning of the class session, an atmosphere of student participation is set that enhances the remainder of the period. Assignments and reports help class members have a better understanding of the subject matter being studied. They also help attendance and punctuality and ensure interest in the session. Several short reports in a single class session give incentive for all to prepare the assigned materials.

The assignment should be made on the basis of the member's ability to prepare and present the report. It should challenge but not frustrate. It is best to present assignments to the students in written form, so both the teacher and the members are sure of the task. And it is important that over a period of time every member of the class participate in one way or another.

The number and kinds of assignments are limitless. It is difficult to make an entire list, since they vary with the purpose of the lesson. Some possibilities are book reviews, memorization, research reports, word definitions, gathering pictures or objects, reading a poem, telling the story of a hymn, gathering background information for a lesson, telling a story, explaining how to use a concordance, preparing a list of test questions, or doing something specific at home, at school, or on the job. Although most assignments should be carefully planned and made by the teacher, often a question, remark, or a discussion during class will prompt a spontaneous assignment.

Teachers must be sure to follow through in calling for the assignment and showing appreciation for the pupil's work. Time should be allotted for the teacher to sum up the information and then continue the session with another method, keeping the purpose of the lesson in mind.

Projects

A project is an extended assignment, usually covering several weeks. It can be one of the most effective teaching methods in that every level of learning is encountered—rote, recognition, restatement, relation, and realization. Usually all five of the physical senses are stimulated at some time during the project. Repeated exposure to the information aids memory and application to the student's life. Jesus used this method when He sent out the Seventy (Luke 10:1-12) and in feeding the multitude (John 6:1-14).

An indirect but important value of projects is the friendly cooperation, fellowship, and involvement with class members outside of the Sunday school class sessions. Involvement can be an answer to the teenage and young adult dropout problem.

Projects are not meant to entertain but are to reinforce the lessons learned. Thus, a project should tie in with the purpose of the unit of study. Ron Held offers these suggestions for using the project method:

> 1. Be sure to plan far enough in advance and make adequate preparation.
> 2. Involve the students in proposing, planning, and carrying out projects. They will take greater responsibility if they feel it is *their* project and not the *teacher's*.
> 3. The teacher serves as a resource person offering advice, information, and encouragement.
> 4. Don't start a project unless you intend to complete it. Let the students know you expect them to finish their projects.[1]

Findley Edge lists the following purposes for different types of projects in which a class may engage:[2]

1. To secure and master certain *information*, such as can be done in connection with a series of lessons. For example, the students could build a model of the tabernacle, or trace the missionary journeys of Paul, the travels of Jesus, or the wanderings of the Israelites. They could also list the references from a concordance or topical Bible on some aspect of doctrine or a principle of Christian life.
2. To change, develop, or deepen certain *attitudes*, such as developing a sensitivity to the needy. The students could arrange for extended interviews with deprived individuals or families.
3. To develop or reinforce certain *habits*, such as regular,

personal Bible reading, prayer, family devotions, family budgeting, or financial faithfulness to God.

4. To render *service* in some area, such as visiting hospitals and institutions, supplying food and other essentials for needy families, preparing missionary boxes, planning an outing for handicapped children, and caring for the homes of the elderly.

Questions and Answers

The question-and-answer method will fail unless the teacher assigns work to the students ahead of the class session. However, if an assignment has been made and the students have been properly motivated to complete the work, the question-and-answer method can be an exciting review and a means of applying those principles to everyday life.

A good question fulfills a purpose, such as preparing the pupils for further study or serving as a source of new information in itself. Key questions should be prepared and written out in advance in a logical order. Questions should be asked in a conversational tone, giving as little information as possible in the question and requiring as much information as possible in the answer. Direct the question to the entire class, then ask a specific person to answer it. Avoid repeating either the question or the answer. Be sure every student has a chance to answer successfully. Ask easy questions first, directing them to the slower pupils so they can succeed. Allow time for the answer; don't be impatient. And be appreciative of whatever answer you receive. Praise develops a feeling of success, and success begets success.

The real test of whether the pupil is learning is his eagerness to ask questions of the teacher. By answering questions from the pupils, the teacher deals with those things the pupils need most. Above all, never bluff an answer. It is better to admit that you do not know the answer and then proceed to find it before the next class session.

A *drill* is an exercise in factual questions, using rote memory. These are *who, what, where,* and *when* questions. To make this exercise fun, divide the class into teams for a short list of rapid-fire, factual questions. Award points for correct answers. A variation is the tic-tac-toe game. One team is "X," and the other is "O." As correct answers are given, team members fill the grid with their marks.

James Dyet offers the following samples of personal-application questions:

> What does this mean to you personally? On the basis of the information contained in this passage of Scripture, how would you advise a person facing the following situation. . . ? What implications do you see here for Christian living? How has this passage of Scripture changed your outlook on life? How will you live differently because of the knowledge you have gained from this study?[3]

Lecture

The lecture is probably the most abused method for teaching youth and adults. We have not placed it at the beginning of this list, because we believe it should rarely be the first method used for teaching a lesson. Once the problem has been clearly defined and interest has been aroused by student activity (such as by an assigned report or questions and answers), then further clarification can be given in a minilecture. When a lecture comes first in a lesson, a tone is set that discourages student participation. How often we have seen a teacher lecture for the first 30 minutes of a class period and then ask, "Does anyone have a question or comment?" Usually such a question is met with an awkward silence, while the teacher gathers his thoughts to finish the class period with a continuation or reiteration of the lecture.

The lecture method has certain advantages. Since the speaker is totally in control, he can present basic concepts in a systematic and well-organized manner, using a minimum of time. It is particularly useful in a large class.

One disadvantage of the lecture method is that it lacks

individual orientation. The absence of student involvement in preparation and participation greatly increases the demands on the teacher's knowledge and speaking abilities. The teacher must know far more about his subject than he can possibly tell in his allotted time. His excitement must keep the lecture alive. Yet, more is needed—for example, a pleasant, well-modulated voice, humor, and some showmanship. Well-prepared overhead transparencies, slides, or a supplemental filmstrip will greatly aid the students' retention of the materials.

When the lecture is used with other teaching methods it is more effective. For example, a lecture can be preceded and followed by a *quiz,* with the same questions on both quizzes. The prequiz gives the students motivation for listening and directs their attention to the points that will be covered. The postquiz summarizes and reinforces the main points. The higher postlecture quiz score gives the students a successful feeling.

A variation of the prelecture and postlecture quiz is *listening teams.* The teacher gives a list of several questions to a few individuals or to teams and asks them to find the answers in his upcoming lecture. The students then summarize the session by their answers. This method is also effective when a movie, filmstrip, or cassette tape is used.

Yet another variety is the *colloquy.* After the lecture, teams of students discuss the information they have just heard and formulate questions for the lecturer. Then one representative from each team forms a panel to direct these questions to the speaker.

A *guest lecturer* adds variety to the class. Caution should be exercised, however, in the selection of a guest. He may know much about his subject, but can he explain it? It may be advisable to ask for an advance outline and offer to prepare overhead transparencies and other teaching aids.

Another lecture variation is the *symposium.* The teacher invites two or more well-informed persons to give brief lectures (about 10 minutes each) related to the lesson or topic. The speakers usually present different aspects or varying attitudes regarding the subject.

A *forum* is planned free time at the end of a lecture for questions, discussion, and dialogue by the audience with the speaker, for the purpose of further clarification and elaboration.

Discussion

The discussion method is probably second only to the lecture in its usage for teaching youth and adults. It holds some of the greatest potential for learning, yet is one of the most abused methods.

Effective classroom discussions require the following elements:

1. *Pupil preparation.* Assignments must be given and completed.
2. *Other background material.* Unless the presession assignment was extensive, rarely can a discussion proceed until information is given on the topic in some form of the lecture method, such as an audiovisual presentation or a report.
3. *A seating arrangement that is conducive to discussion.* While discussion is not impossible when the students are seated in rows, it is much easier while seated around tables or in a semicircle.
4. *An atmosphere of close fellowship among the students.* The students need to feel free to respond with informal spontaneity. Conscious efforts must be made to help the students feel like closely knit friends.
5. *A classroom atmosphere of active student involvement in the teaching/learning process.* If the class period begins with a lecture, the tone is set for a teacher-dominated session.
6. *A well-planned discussion pattern.* The teacher needs preplanned, clear questions that will lead the discussion toward a solution of the problem in a logical sequence.

7. *Time control.* This keeps the discussion lively and on target, while allowing for a satisfactory conclusion in the time allocated for this part of the lesson.

8. *Arrival at a conclusion.* The teacher must summarize the group's opinions and make a satisfactory life application with the Biblical principle clearly in focus.

One other necessary ingredient in the discussion method is the participation of all the students. This requires that the teacher tactfully limit those who would dominate the discussion, while drawing out the more reserved. Here are a few variations of the discussion method that will aid the resourceful teacher in this task:

The *circle response* calls for input from each member of the class, going from pupil to pupil. No person may speak a second time until everyone has spoken once. Of course, no one should be forced to respond.

Brainstorming may be done by the entire class or in small groups of three or more. A problem is described by the teacher, and the pupils respond with ideas—any ideas. Even if the thought seems silly, the teacher should write it down. Later the ideas can be screened for appropriateness.

Buzz groups are small discussion groups. The teacher can assign either the same topic or a different one to each buzz group. Ideas are recorded during the discussion (5 to 8 minutes), and then a spokesman from each group reports back to the entire class.

Dyads or "couple buzzers" are a variation of the buzz group; there are only two members in each group. When pupils are seated in rows or pews, or when the problem posed by the teacher requires only a minute or two of group discussion, dyads can be used effectively.

A *panel* is an informal discussion by two or more students seated at the front of the class. Each panel member covers a particular aspect of the topic.

Testing

Memory is enhanced by repeated recall of material. For this

reason, the teacher should frequently review within each lesson, and occasionally give a five- or six-question quiz at the end of the lesson. A review quiz on the preceding week's lesson can reinforce the building blocks for the current week's materials. It is important that testing is thought of as a method of *teaching,* designed to aid the teaching/learning process, and not as a judgmental tool.

Whereas most youth are accustomed to tests, many adults fear them. Test results should never be used as a source of embarrassment. In fact, tests should be mostly for the students' own use in the learning process.

Writing and Drama

Students can compose poems, songs, and prayers. Almost any student can write a comparison of two Biblical characters or keep a diary of his spiritual growth. With a little imagination a student can write a newspaper account of David's triumph over the Philistine giant, or create a daily log that Paul may have written as he was journeying toward Rome. An inventive student can write a modern-day parable. Letters sent to missionaries are both encouraging to those in foreign lands and an aid to further student involvement with the missionaries.

Any youth or adult student can *roleplay.* Findley Edge defines roleplaying as "an adaptation of . . . 'make believe play,' in which the class may observe various attitudes expressed and evaluate the consequences of those attitudes. It is a brief, spontaneous, unrehearsed presentation of a problem in which certain members of the class act out certain roles. There is no script prepared, no memorizing of parts."[4]

Attitudes Toward Teaching Methods

If youth or adult students have become accustomed to only one or two teaching methods, such as discussion or lecture, their initial response to other methods will probably be discouraging. If you are genuinely interested in improving your teaching and are willing to try methods to enhance the teaching/learning process, make only gradual changes in your style. Your students have taken several years becoming accustomed to the current methods. Give them a few months to become comfortable with methods that involve them.

---

[1]Ronald G. Held, *Learning Together* (Springfield, MO: Gospel Publishing House, 1976), p. 67.

[2]Adapted from Findley B. Edge, *Helping the Teacher* (Nashville, TN: Broadman Press, 1959), pp. 128,129.

[3]James T. Dyet, *Getting Through to Adults* (Denver, CO: Accent-B/P Publications, Inc., 1980), p. 93.

[4]Edge, *Helping the Teacher,* p. 114.

9

Lesson Preparation and Evaluation

> And beginning at . . . the prophets, he expounded unto them in all the Scriptures the things concerning himself (Luke 24:27).

We who have been called to and gifted for this ministry of teaching have responded with commitment and preparation. We have studied the general characteristics of our pupils and have observed their individual needs. Understanding how learning takes place and the teacher's role in that process, we have studied the tools of our "trade" and comprehend many of the methods for using them. All this comes into focus in the preparation for each lesson and its teaching. The goal is to produce mature Christians. Every lesson should be aimed at this ultimate achievement.

Lesson Preparation

Each Sunday school lesson must be an impartation of divine truths that have been made real to the teacher. Daily prayer and reading of God's Word allow communication to flow between the Master and His servant. Both the teacher's personal needs and those of his students come into focus as he allows the Holy Spirit to guide. Prayer for pupils should be specific. Try using a prayer-request list in these times of intercession.

As soon as a teacher receives the next quarter's lesson materials, he should preview them. Previewing the lessons early allows time to plan special assignments or projects, gather materials for special teaching methods, and master and assimilate the materials so they can be taught from the heart as well as from the head. Usually a quarterly of lessons has a general theme and purpose. An early overview allows the teacher to see each lesson as a part of that general 3-month goal. Precept is added to precept until another facet of Christian maturity has been fashioned with an unshakable structure.

How often have teachers said on Saturday night as they are preparing the next day's lesson, "Next week I will begin preparing earlier!"

It is almost impossible to teach from one's heart a lesson that was seen for the first time less than 24 hours earlier. It is far better to study for 30 minutes *every* day of the week than to cram for even 4 hours on Saturday night.

The following is a suggested daily preparation schedule:[1]

Sunday—Read the Bible story or passage.
Monday—Read the quarterly and other materials.
Tuesday—Develop the lesson goal and a preliminary outline.
Wednesday—Plan methods and learning activities.
Thursday—Secure teaching supplies.
Friday—Write a final teaching plan.
Saturday—Review all materials.

Let us turn to a day-by-day discussion of this preparation schedule.

Sunday—Read the Bible Story or Passage

This involves not just a few verses, but the entire chapter, or possibly several chapters. Discover the time and setting for this passage. Refer to a Bible dictionary, commentary, Bible atlas, and other books, as they are available. Check with other teachers or your pastor if you need additional help.

Monday—Read the Quarterly and Other Materials

Not only should the teacher's quarterly be read, but also any teaching aid packets that may be available, the student quarterly, and any student workbooks that are being used.

Tuesday—(1)Develop a Lesson Aim or Goal

What is a lesson aim or goal? It is "a statement of what the teacher wants to have happen in the life of the student as a result of the lesson study."[2]

Without a lesson goal, the teacher may try to cover too much material, ramble aimlessly, fail to relate to the pupil's needs, and/or see little life change. On the other hand, a lesson goal helps the teacher to find direction in the learning process, develop a proper sequence of class activities, and determine what methods and materials should be used. Finally, a lesson goal serves as a basis for lesson evaluation. One cannot judge whether he has reached his goal if he did not know in the first place where he wanted to go.

A good lesson aim or goal has three characteristics: It will be concise enough to be written in a few words. It will be specific, attainable, and measurable. It will be flexible, so that it can be personalized to the needs of the pupils being taught.

The ultimate goal of the ministry of teaching is to develop students into mature Christians (Ephesians 4:13). To accomplish this aim, we must move from the pupil's "felt" needs to his "real" needs. There is always an area where the Word of God overlaps the needs of life. It is at this overlapping area that lessons must be aimed; meeting human need with the principles of Holy Writ.

Lesson goals direct the teaching/learning process toward one of three major directions: A knowledge goal, an attitude or feeling goal, or a conduct or doing goal. Findley B. Edge says:

> If the teacher is to secure more results either in the amount of Bible knowledge learned, or in terms of attitudes deepened, or in terms of Christian living, he must select one of these aims, and only one, *for a given lesson,* and seek only that one with all his heart.[3]

Before an attitude change can be effected, knowledge must be present; before conduct is determined by spiritual precepts, both knowledge and attitude must have been learned. Christian maturity implies a change of conduct. Knowledge alone does not make Christians. Even Satan uses the Word of God (Luke 4:10). But conduct will never be changed without a knowledge of His Word. Even attitude alone is not enough: "The devils also believe, and tremble. But wilt thou know, O vain man, that faith without works is dead?" (James 2:19,20).

Tuesday—(2)Develop a Preliminary Outline

The first part of Tuesday's lesson preparation assignment is to develop a lesson goal, which guides all other preparation and the teaching of the lesson itself. The remainder of Tuesday's work is that of developing a preliminary outline.

As with almost any public speaking, the lesson should have an introduction or approach, a body, and a conclusion or application. The purpose of the approach is to arouse interest, involve the students, and lead into the lesson. Most importantly, the introduction must identify a "felt" student need, and link the meeting of that need to the lesson. The body presents the knowledge, desired attitude, or conduct response toward which the entire lesson is aimed. The conclusion summarizes, reviews, or calls for action, depending on the lesson's goal.

This outline must be the teacher's. It cannot be an outline of the quarterly material, because some of the teaching ideas given in the teacher's helps will not apply to a given class situation.

Wednesday—Plan Methods and Learning Activities

The goal of the lesson largely determines the methods to be used in the teaching/learning process. The approach or introduction might employ the use of a startling statement, a series of questions, or a brief anecdote. Student activity, such as brainstorming, can be used to help the students think about and discover needs that can be met by this lesson.

If the lesson goal is knowledge, use methods such as a lecture, an assignment and report, questions and answers, and a practice and drill. If the goal is attitude, use methods that provide emotional experiences, such as stories, testimonials, pictures, and music. If the goal is conduct response, the methods may include panels, discussions, personal-application questions and answers, and project assignments and reports.

The conclusion, too, is determined by the lesson goal. If the goal is knowledge, the conclusion can be a brief review or quiz. If it is attitude, use a song or prayers. If the objective is conduct response, ask for a written resolve with a plan of action.

Other considerations in choosing a method should be the class' age-level, the pupils' background in the Bible and Sunday school, your own skills with various methods, the amount of time you have to teach the lesson, and the classroom facilities. What works well in one situation may not work at all in another class.

Thursday—Secure Teaching Supplies

Thursday is far too late to order a filmstrip, record, or movie. This should be done at the beginning of the quarter by the church's media center coordinator (unless this material is already in the center). But other materials can now be prepared. Duplicate any worksheets and quizzes, and purchase handwork supplies. Any part of the handwork that must be done by the teacher should be completed on Thursday. Collect flannelgraph materials, pictures, maps, illustrations, overhead transparencies, and demonstrations, and make certain that all are in proper order.

Friday—Write a Final Teaching Plan

Take time on Friday to rewrite the lesson goal and preliminary outline that you prepared on Tuesday. Include the teaching methods and learning activities that will best reach the lesson goal. Include in this plan the supplies collected yesterday. By now the lesson is coming from the heart. The teacher can hardly wait for Sunday to convey the message that God has given!

One new ingredient should be added today—a time schedule. In the lesson plan, write the starting time for the "lesson approach." Don't forget to allow sufficient time for any "prelesson" activities. Then write beside each point of the lesson body what time it will begin. Finally, write a time by the concluding part of the lesson. Without these time guides, the class period will be over and the "punch lines" will be missed.

Saturday—Review All Materials

Review your teaching supplies, methods, and outline, and pray again for God's anointing as you minister tomorrow. Believe for conversions and decisions for Christ as you prepare. Believe that Christians will be matured in the faith.

Sample Lesson Plan for a Junior Class[4]

Quarter's theme: "God's Faithfulness"

Quarter's aim: To help the students realize how great and faithful God is.

Lesson theme: God's faithfulness in hearing and answering prayer.

Scripture passage: 1 Kings 3:5-14

Major truth taught in passage: God heard and answered Solomon's prayer.

Pupils' needs to be met by lesson:

1. To feel confident that God hears our prayers.
2. To realize that God is powerful, answering prayers.
3. To discover the value of prayer in personal lives.

Lesson goal: Knowledge—to realize that God hears and answers the prayers of His obedient children.

Schedule:

9:15-9:30 (Before class begins)—Check the roll as each student enters the classroom. Ask each one to write a short paragraph telling about one of his recent prayers that God has answered.

9:30-9:35—*Introduction:* Have volunteers read the paragraphs they wrote.

9:35-9:45—*Body of the lesson:* Tell the story contained in the Scripture passage, relating it to the lesson theme and goal.

9:45-9:50—Scripture memorization: James 5:16.

9:50-10:00—Divide the class into three small groups.

Group #1: Using a concordance, discover how many times prayer is mentioned in the Bible.

Group #2: Using a Bible dictionary, discover the meaning of prayer.

Group #3: Using the Bible, read Matthew 6:9-13, to discover the method of prayer.

10:00-10:05—Have each group report back to the class.

10:05-10:10—Have each student write a request for which he will pray throughout the coming week.

10:10-10:15—*Conclusion:* Lead in prayer. Students may also volunteer to pray sentence prayers.

Evaluation

When planning a trip, we first note on the map where we are now and where we want to go. Next, we chart the best way to travel between those two points and estimate the amount of time the trip will take. We decide how much money we will need for fuel and meals along the way. As we make the trip, we check the miles traveled, the time taken, and the fuel used, against our previous estimates to determine our progress. We may decide that we can stop for a relaxing refreshment, or we may learn that we must keep moving, since we are a little behind schedule.

Much the same process should be true in the teaching/learning process. If goals are not set and progress is not continually evaluated, little will be accomplished. Henrietta Mears said: "The teacher has not taught until the pupil has learned." The students learning is the measure of the teacher's success. Three kinds of evaluation are necessary: self-evaluation; evaluation by others, such as superiors; and evaluation as measured by the students' progress toward Christian maturity.

Self-evaluation and Evaluation by Others

Because evaluations are almost always subjective, they cannot be totally accurate. They indicate general characteristics; particularly if an evaluation made by one person is compared to that made by another. Trends of development are measurable if evaluation forms are saved and compared to those made in subsequent years.

It is desirable for Sunday school administrators to spend less time in the office during the Sunday school hour and more time in the classrooms doing evaluations and learning ways to improve the Christian education process. Their other Sunday morning tasks should be delegated.

The attitudes of both the teacher and the administrator toward the subject of evaluation are extremely important. The administrator must be considered a minister (a servant) to the teacher, rather than his judge. The purpose of an evaluation is solely to improve what is already a good process.

Each teacher should do a self-evaluation and then compare his opinions with the administrator's. This should reveal both positive characteristics and those that can be improved. The evaluation forms should be completed once a year, jointly discussed, and then filed for future reference. As the evaluation process is repeated year after year, an accurate picture develops and progress will be seen.

The evaluation form on the next page could be used for this purpose:

Teacher Evaluation Form[5]

Completed for (name of teacher) ______________________________

Completed by ____

Ratings to be used: 4-Excellent; 3-Good; 2-Fair; 1-Poor

Personal Characteristics

____ 1. Appearance
____ 2. Poise
____ 3. Neatness
____ 4. Promptness
____ 5. Creativity
____ 6. Enthusiasm
____ 7. Initiative
____ 8. Tact
____ 9. Sense of humor
____ 10. Cooperativeness
____ 11. Leadership
____ 12. Friendliness
____ 13. Voice quality
____ 14. Use of correct English
____ 15. Ability to communicate

Teaching Abilities

____ 16. Knowledge of Bible content
____ 17. Knowledge of resource materials
____ 18. Interest in teaching
____ 19. Knowledge of the learning process
____ 20. Knowledge of teaching skills
____ 21. Awareness of pupils' needs
____ 22. Effective planning
____ 23. Securing pupils' interest
____ 24. Holding pupils' attention
____ 25. Motivating learning
____ 26. Use of teaching methods
____ 27. Use of teaching materials
____ 28. Use of audiovisual aids
____ 29. Control of class
____ 30. Understanding of pupils' differences

Total points _____ (Key: 91-120, excellent; 61-90, good; 31-60, fair; 0-30, poor.)

Evaluation by the Students' Progress

The most accurate evaluation of a teacher's effectiveness is a measurement of the students' progress toward Christian maturity, which is difficult but not impossible to measure. The first step is to establish a base. Then, periodic measurements can be taken and filed in each student's folder. This year's form must be completed *before* last year's form is reviewed, to avoid prejudicing.

As these forms are completed, filed, reviewed, and compared from year to year, the teacher will see not only the student's progress (whereby his teaching can be evaluated), but also the student's weaknesses or needs (which should be addressed in the next year's lessons).

The following forms can be used for measuring the students' Christian maturity:

Observation of a Preschool or Elementary Child

Name ______________________________ Date ________________
Name of observer _________ Time observed ______ to ________

1. Make note of any statements or responses by the child that would indicate his feelings toward:
God ____
Jesus ____
Church ____
The Bible ____
His friends ____

2. Make note of the following during Bible storytime:
Does the child appear to listen? ____________________
What seems to attract the child most? ______________
Does he seem to grasp the meaning of the story? __________
What behavior indicates this? _______________________
Comments ____

3. Make note of the following during worship time:
What is the child's response toward coming to the worship area? ____

What is the child's participation in worship? ______
Comments ______

4. Make note of the following sometime during the observation session:

What *physical development* do you observe in this child?
Are there apparent *physical needs* that you observe?
What *emotional development* do you observe in this child?
Are there apparent *emotional needs* that you observe?
What *social development* do you observe in this child?
Are there apparent *social needs* that you observe?
What *spiritual development* do you observe in this child?
Are there apparent *spiritual needs* that you observe?

Observation of a Youth or Adult Student

Name ______ Date ______
Name of observer ______ Time observed ______ to ______

1. *Relationship to Christ:*

Does he appear to understand the plan of salvation? ______
Has he accepted Christ as his personal Saviour? ______
Has he been baptized in water? ______
Has he been baptized in the Holy Spirit? ______
How does he evidence that his life is committed to Christ? ______

2. *Spiritual Growth:*

Does he engage in Bible study outside of class? ______
Does he take time for personal devotions? ______
Is he applying Biblical truths in his life? ______
Is he developing a Christian life-style? ______
Is he sharing his faith in Christ with others? ______
Is he learning to be a good steward of his resources, time, and abilities? ______

3. *Church Involvement:*

Is the pupil faithful in his attendance at Sunday school and church? ______
Does he seem to enjoy these activities? ______
Does he take part in out-of-class activities? ______
Does he bring his friends to Sunday school and church? ______

Is he assuming class and church responsibilities? ___________
Does he speak well of the class and the church? _____________

4. *Bible and Doctrinal Knowledge:*

Does he have an adequate understanding of the Bible for his age? ____

Can he explain the basic doctrines of salvation, healing, the Baptism, and the Second Coming?____________________

Is he growing in his Bible-study skills?_________________

5. *Attitude and Action:*

Does he show a willingness to change when necessary? ______
Does he have negative attitudes which hinder his maturation?
Is he consistently evaluating his own life in the light of God's Word? ____

Obviously, these forms cannot be completed solely from classroom observation. The answers to many questions will be found in ongoing out-of-the-classroom teacher/pupil relationships.

Any of the evaluation forms suggested in this chapter may be reproduced for your own use. To conserve pages in this text, little space was given for written answers to the questions. As you retype them, allow for additional answer lines.

---

[1]"Lesson Preparation," *Staff Training Series* (Springfield, MO: Gospel Publishing House, 1980).

[2]*Ibid.*

[3]Findley B. Edge, *Helping the Teacher* (Nashville: Broadman Press, 1959), p. 13.

[4]D. V. Hurst, *Mastering the Methods* (Springfield, MO: Gospel Publishing House, 1979), pp. 84,85.

[5]*Ibid.*, p. 95.

10

Expanding the Ministry of Teaching

> After these things the Lord appointed other seventy also, and sent them two and two before his face into every city and place, whither he himself would come (Luke 10:1).

As the church has been likened to the human body (1 Corinthians 12:14-27), so is the Sunday school. It is a living, vibrant organism that requires nourishment and exercise and is constantly growing and expanding. When cells die, they are replaced with new ones.

This chapter is a potpourri of evangelistic programs and concepts that give the Sunday school and our ministries of teaching opportunities for growth and expansion.

Expansion Programs

First, let us consider three children's outreach programs: the cradle roll, vacation Bible school, and neighborhood Bible clubs.

Cradle Roll

The cradle roll is more than a poster hanging on the back wall of the auditorium, displaying the pictures of the church's babies. Its function goes beyond that of simply providing a baby-sitting service for the parents of those babies. Of course, church families do appreciate having their babies lovingly cared for while they attend the adult services, but the cradle roll is also an effective arm of outreach into the community. Immediately following a baby's birth, parents who have previously given little thought to spiritual matters are often very receptive. They are especially aware that they need help in knowing how to train their child.

Neighborhood canvassing, birth announcements in the newspaper, newcomer lists from the Welcome Wagon, and regular calls to diaper service firms can produce prospects for your cradle roll. Visits should be made in the home of every prospect by someone from this department. After the baby's enrollment, these home contacts should continue, especially if the parents are not yet regularly attending the services. Through literature, conversation, and continued prayer, the parents will be impressed with their responsibility for providing spiritual training for their family.

New mothers appreciate meeting informally in a home setting to discuss mutual concerns and have a brief Bible study. Unchurched mothers can be reached who might not otherwise attend church services. Several times during the year, schedule a social at the church or in a home where the mothers and fathers of the cradle roll children can have a time of fellowship.

On Cradle Roll Sunday, which is the second Sunday of March, the importance of the baby in the home and the responsibilities of the parents should be emphasized. Present the new babies to the church and ask the pastor to pray for them, their parents, and their teachers.

Challenge an adult class to furnish some of the equipment needed in the nursery. Supplying crib sheets, bottle warmers, and toys, and laundering the linens each week are a great assistance. Parents are influenced by the cleanliness, cheerfulness, and adequate staffing of the nursery. These factors may determine whether visiting parents decide to become regular members.

Vacation Bible School

Vacation Bible school is an evangelistic outreach of the church. Traditionally, it has been conducted during 2 weeks of the summer in either the morning or afternoon. It is attended by grade school children who come to the church facilities for the daily sessions. However, the flexibility of the VBS has allowed it to go through many changes, so that today the program and schedule have been adapted to meet every possible situation and facility.

Anytime can be VBS time. The summer months are still the most popular, since more workers are available then. High school and college students make excellent workers, as do public or private school teachers. Choose a time when the maximum number of workers are available in your area.

Adapt the schedule to fit your situation. The 2-week schedule can be changed to 1 week or even 1 or 2 days a week for 5 weeks. Many churches find that an evening VBS offers several advantages. Workers who have daytime employment are available to assist, and the evening hours are best for a family VBS.

No longer is it necessary to conduct the VBS in the church. Successful endeavors have been held in the recreation rooms of condominiums and apartment complexes, community halls, private school buildings, YMCA facilities, recreation rooms of industrial parks, and vacant stores of shopping centers. Sometimes it is easier to go where the children are than to bring them to the church.

Consider VBS as a missionary opportunity—not only a time to provide concentrated Bible study for the churched, but also a chance to reach the unchurched with the gospel of Jesus Christ and bring them to a decision and personal commitment. Follow up on those who are not already regularly attending a Sunday school. Encourage those who make decisions for Christ by visiting them at their home. Often an entire family is won to the Lord and the church because such interest is shown.

Positive outgrowth occurs when previously untrained workers volunteer to serve apprenticeships during VBS, learning from their "master" teacher. After further training, they too can teach on a regular basis in the Sunday school.

A VBS evaluation session is necessary to set goals and

determine what adaptations should be made for next year's campaign.

Neighborhood Bible Clubs

Neighborhood Bible clubs, or backyard Bible clubs as they are sometimes called, usually meet for up to 1½ hours each weekday, or a special effort can be limited to only 1 or 2 weeks. They are conducted in a yard, basement, garage, living room, family room, or patio—any place that is relatively quiet, comfortable, and free of distractions. The club can meet any time in the day that is convenient for the hostess and the grade school children who attend.

Some high school and college students give their entire summer to neighborhood Bible clubs. Junior high boys and girls sometimes assist with song leading, crafts, and caring for the small children of the adult workers.

To determine the location of your Bible club, consider the areas where there is a concentration of church families. Conduct a club for one age-group at each home. For example, the first through third graders could attend at one home, while the fourth through sixth graders could meet at another. Ten to fifteen children with two or three workers can comfortably meet in this type of setting. Include songs, prayer, a Bible story, and a memory verse. Crafts are optional.

Canvass the neighborhood to promote the club. A clown or other novelty character walking the neighborhood streets attracts children's attention. Talk personally with parents, informing them of your plans. You may wish to adapt a VBS curriculum for use in the Bible club. The Gospel Publishing House or a local Christian bookstore can help supply other materials.

Expansion Concepts

Now, let us consider several outreach concepts, such as open enrollment, friendship "webs" or fellowship groups, an expanded concept of Sunday school, and the discipling of new teachers.

Open Enrollment

Many Sunday schools still demand that a person attend three consecutive Sundays before he can become a part of the Sunday school. Why? Because they are following a tradition so old that even research has been unable to determine its origin. The Assemblies of God "Sunday School Guidelines" recommends that a person be enrolled the first Sunday he attends Sunday school and/or expresses an interest in it. These guidelines also recommend that no one be removed from the enrollment list unless he dies, moves from the community, requests to be removed, or is known to be *regularly* attending another church. The irregular attenders should *not* be placed on a "casual list," but should be kept where they will receive the most effort and exposure to the ministries of the church.

We could not number the individuals who have been offended by their removal from a Sunday school roll. Often the reason for their absence was unavoidable on their part—extended illness, travel, work, or parents who would not or could not bring their children to Sunday school. There are likewise many who have "given up" trying to become part of a Sunday school because they could not attend three consecutive Sundays—the requirement for being accepted. This is especially true of children from broken homes where the courts may order that they spend a certain number of weekends in the noncustodial parent's home.

The purpose of Sunday school enrollment should not be confused with church membership. Sunday school enrollment represents a commitment on the part of the *church.* Church membership, in contrast, requires a commitment on the part of the *individual.*

Attendance usually remains constant at around 60 to 80 percent of the enrollment. Trimming the rolls soon has a downward effect on attendance. Likewise, adding new persons to the roll causes attendance to increase.

It is recommended that anyone who wishes to be enrolled should be, whether or not he has ever attended Sunday school.

Once the principle of open enrollment is established, challenge individuals to enroll friends and acquaintances. Converts can be immediately enrolled in Bible study. Also, teachers should ask visitors if they would like to be enrolled. Once or twice a year, the Sunday school may recruit and train teams of workers to canvass the community, enrolling those who desire to become a part of a regular Bible study.

Before a concerted effort is launched to enroll a group of new persons, certain groundwork must be done. Is there adequate space to add several more people? Will we need to form new classes? Is the staff prepared and trained for teaching those with little Bible knowledge? Is there a well thought-out plan of follow-up? Greeters and ushers may need training. And the entire congregation must be made to feel responsible to see that newcomers are comfortable and made to feel welcome and wanted.

Friendship "Webs" and Fellowship Groups

The Early Church grew primarily through relationships between family members, neighbors, friends, and servants.

> Indeed, a solid case can be presented that Paul's strategy for establishing churches was, in large part, to find responsive people, convert them, and then reach others in the new converts' webs of relationships. Responsiveness was found as the gospel spread through the webs of family, friends, and associates.[1]

According to Dr. Win Arn, the natural and normal way that churches grow is through *oikos,* or "household" or friendship evangelism. Today, *oikos* evangelism is still the primary source of conversions in the United States. Over 10,000 people were asked, "What was responsible for your coming to Christ and this church?" "The influence of a friend or relative" was the response given by 70 to 90 percent.[2]

The people who are most responsive to Sunday school outreach efforts are found within the webs of members who are presently attending. When new persons come into the Sunday school, untapped webs are opened; consisting of individuals, family members, and friends outside the church and Sunday school.

According to the Institute for American Church Growth, the average believer has 8.4 contacts of unchurched friends, relatives, associates, and neighbors. Newer Christians average 12 contacts, but the longer a person has been a believer the fewer unchurched contacts he has. Enormous possibilities are available to most Sunday schools if they will build a prospect list composed of these people.

Strive to win entire family units. Family members are often very responsive to members of their own family, particularly if the father is won. If the family is not won, the possibilities of one family member eventually dropping out of church increase tremendously.

Fellowship groups are closely related to the basic principle of "friendship webs." However, the fellowship group (sometimes called a cell, zone, or home Bible-study group) goes beyond fellowship into other ministries that can be very effective in small, neighborhood meetings.

Fellowship group meetings provide a means for systematic Bible study in each neighborhood. Of course, the pastor must choose the group leaders, plan the Bible studies, and teach these studies to the leaders before each set of scheduled meetings. This leadership multiplication delegates responsibility to the laity and directly involves them, which is another advantage of the Sunday school.

Within the context of a home Bible study, the congregation's faith is exhibited not only in the church, but also in the community. Many people will attend a home Bible study before they will attend a church service. Time is available in home meetings for prayer concerning specific, individual needs. In such a climate of prayer, opportunity is given for members to be saved, baptized in the Holy Spirit, receive physical healing, and exercise spiritual gifts. Each person has an opportunity to become a functioning part of the body of Christ.

It is not advisable to enter this ministry too rapidly. Begin with only a few fellowship groups, and do not expect the entire congregation to participate. Some will like the idea, while others will reject it entirely.

A Broadened Concept of "Sunday School"

At one time in the United States, the railroads were our primary means of transportation. Now very few people ride the trains. Instead, the airlines provide our primary public transportation. Consequently, the railroads have become a much less dominant financial force in our economy.

What if the railroads had thought of themselves not as railroads but as "people movers," and when the airplane was invented, they had invested some of their capital holdings into its development? Today we might be flying the Gulf, Mobil, and Ohio airlines, instead of Eastern.

The huge oil corporations have learned this lesson, and now see themselves as being not in the oil business, but in the energy business. Thus, they are buying coal mines, solar equipment manufacturing companies, etc.

The Sunday school is in the Christian education "business." In the last 10 to 20 years, innovations have presented themselves, such as Royal Rangers, Missionettes, home fellowship groups, weeknight Bible courses, etc. The Sunday school can either consider these as encroachments upon its "monopoly" in the field of Christian education, or it can view them as expansions of its work. The former view will result in the Sunday school's outdating and demise, while the latter view will enhance the total educational process.

A more realistic approach is to coordinate the total educational efforts of the church. We advise periodic meetings of the Sunday school staff, Royal Rangers, Missionettes, fellowship group leaders, and pastoral staff to coordinate the educational thrust. For example, every one of these teaching teams will be better equipped by simply knowing what subjects the other teams will be covering in the upcoming quarter.

Discipling Others for Your Ministry

There is one goal that every Sunday school teacher should make his own. And that is to begin discipling (training) someone to take his place. Workers are easier to recruit to a position of training rather than immediately working. Trainees have time to assess the responsibility and determine if they want it. They can become comfortable in that area of ministry and be thoroughly trained for it.

Once a person has been discipled for a ministry, he may assume the leadership of the master teacher's class. If the master teacher is not ready to move into another area of involvement, the newly trained worker can go into the community and recruit his own class of students. This results in a growing Sunday school taught by qualified instructors.

This idea is valid not only for Sunday school teachers, but also for all church workers—musicians, vocalists, deacons, custodians, secretaries, etc. Moses discipled Joshua to lead the Children of Israel after his death (Deuteronomy 3:28). David had another trained to tend the sheep while he was away slaying the Philistine giant (1 Samuel 17:20). Elijah discipled Elisha so well that when Elijah was translated, Elisha received a *double* portion of the spirit that had been on his master teacher (2 Kings 2:9-11). Paul carefully trained Timothy and instructed him to commit these teachings "to faithful men, who shall be able to teach others also" (2 Timothy 2:2).

If we disciple others for areas of ministry and delegate authority to them, that authority must be accountable to God-ordained overseers. A Sunday school teacher should be recruited to a specific job description and agreement. Recordkeeping should measure a teacher's performance against the standard. If the job performance meets or exceeds expectations, an award should be given. If the performance is below expectations, the reasons must be discovered, so that assistance and further training can be given. In either case, appreciation is very much in order. The key factor is *regular* accountability. Without it, neither the Sunday school nor its workers will reach their potential.

An Encounter With God

The apostle Paul wrote in Romans 12:2: "And be not conformed to this world: but be ye transformed by the renewing of your mind, that ye may prove what is that good, and acceptable, and perfect will of God." The word "transformed" is translated from the Greek word *metamorphoo,* from which we get the English word *metamorphosis,* the process by which a tadpole becomes a frog or a caterpillar becomes a butterfly. It is the same Greek word that is translated "transfigured" in Matthew 17:2—the record of Jesus' transfiguration.

Before a caterpillar becomes a butterfly, it must spin a cocoon around itself. It must isolate itself from the rest of the world, so that a transformation can take place.

The apostle Peter was willing to "cocoon" himself in the Upper Room until "the day of Pentecost was fully come" (Acts 2:1). It was then that this formerly spiritually weak apostle stood and proclaimed, "This is that which was spoken by the prophet Joel" (Acts 2:16)!

The night before the deceiver Jacob was to see his long-estranged brother, Esau, he was desperate for a blessing from God. If you will, he "cocooned" himself at Peniel, wrestling with "a man . . . until the breaking of the day" (Genesis 32:24). The man said, "Let me go, for the day breaketh. And he [Jacob] said, I will not let thee go, except thou bless me" (Genesis 32:26).

If we could leave any one message of admonition with the Sunday school workers who read this text, it would be this: *Encounter God!* "Cocoon" yourself with God until you are totally "transfigured" in mind and spirit by His life-changing power! Don't let God go until He blesses you!

Isaiah saw God "high and lifted up" (Isaiah 6:1). But then the prophet truly encountered God:

> Then flew one of the seraphim unto me, having a live coal in his hand, which he had taken with the tongs from off the altar: and he laid it upon my mouth, and said, Lo, this hath touched thy lips; and thine iniquity is taken away, and thy sin purged. Also I heard the voice of the Lord, saying, Whom shall I send, and who will go for us? Then said I, Here am I; send me (Isaiah 6:6-8).

God has called, ordained, and specially gifted us for the ministry of teaching. It is a supernatural gift that is intended to reap spiritual results; bringing growth and maturity to the body of Christ. As ministers, we are servants, addressing ourselves to the needs that we can meet with our special abilities. We have committed ourselves to this ministry until we finish the work He has given us to do. For this ministry, we have prepared ourselves and we continually prepare.

Now may we so *encounter God* that when He asks, "Whom shall I send and who will go for us?" we will fervently reply, "Here am I; send me."

---

[1]Charles Arn, Donald McGavran, and Win Arn, *Growth, A New Vision for the Sunday School* (Pasadena, CA: Church Growth Press, 1980), p. 73.

[2]*Ibid.*, p. 76.

Bibliography

Arn, Charles; McGavran, Donald; and Arn, Win. *Growth, A New Vision for the Sunday School.* Pasadena, CA: Church Growth Press, 1980.

Brown, Opal. *Fun With Handcraft.* Grand Rapids: Baker Book House, 1975.

Dobbins, Dr. Richard D. *Train up a Child.* Stow, OH: Creative Communications, 1973.

Dobson, Dr. James. *Hide or Seek.* Old Tappan, NJ: Fleming H. Revell Co., 1974.

Dyet, James T. *Getting Through to Adults.* Denver: Accent-B/P Publications, Inc., 1980.

Fillmore, Donna. *Let's Teach With Bible Games.* Grand Rapids: Baker Book House, 1978.

Hurston, John W., and Hurston, Karen L. *Caught in the Web.* Seoul, Korea: Church Growth International, 1977.

Hutton, Dolores K. *Sunday School Activities for Preschool Children.* Grand Rapids: Baker Book House, 1979.

Jones, Elizabeth B. *Teaching Primaries Today.* Grand Rapids: Baker Book House, 1974.

Latham, Joy. *Living and Learning With Nursery Children.* Grand Rapids: Baker Book House, 1975.

Prichard, Pamela R. *How to Conduct Backyard Bible Clubs.* Chicago: Moody Press, 1977.

Richards, Lawrence O. *You the Teacher.* Chicago: Moody Press, 1972.

Sanner, A. Elwood, and Harper, A. F. *Exploring Christian Education.* Kansas City: Beacon Hill Press, 1978.

Self, Margaret M. *Effective Year-Round Bible Ministries.* Glendale, CA: G/L Regal Publications, 1980.

Tozer, A. W. *The Pursuit of God.* Harrisburg, PA: Christian Publications, Inc., 1948.

Weising, Edward F., and Weising, Gwen. *Singleness—An Opportunity for Growth and Fulfillment.* Springfield, MO: Gospel Publishing House, 1982.

White, Marian. *Bible-Teaching Finger Plays.* Grand Rapids: Baker Book House, 1977.

Wienecke, J. Melton. *Tools That Teach.* Grand Rapids: Baker Book House, 1973.

Williamson, Nancy S. *100 Handy Ideas for Busy Teachers.* Grand Rapids: Baker Book House, 1980.

Zuck, Roy B., and Benson, Warren S. *Youth Education in the Church.* Chicago: Moody Press, 1978.

Zuck, Roy B., and Clark, Robert E. *Childhood Education in the Church.* Chicago: Moody Press, 1975.

Zuck, Roy B., and Getz, Gene A. *Adult Education in the Church.* Chicago: Moody Press, 1975.